Translation and Multilingual Natural Language Processing

Editors: Oliver Czulo (Universität Leipzig), Silvia Hansen-Schirra (Johannes Gutenberg-Universität Mainz), Reinhard Rapp (Johannes Gutenberg-Universität Mainz)

In this series:

1. Fantinuoli, Claudio & Federico Zanettin (eds.). New directions in corpus-based translation studies.
2. Hansen-Schirra, Silvia & Sambor Grucza (eds.). Eyetracking and Applied Linguistics.
3. Neumann, Stella, Oliver Čulo & Silvia Hansen-Schirra (eds.). Annotation, exploitation and evaluation of parallel corpora: TC3 I.
4. Czulo, Oliver & Silvia Hansen-Schirra (eds.). Crossroads between Contrastive Linguistics, Translation Studies and Machine Translation: TC3 II.
5. Rehm, Georg, Felix Sasaki, Daniel Stein & Andreas Witt (eds.). Language technologies for a multilingual Europe: TC3 III.
6. Menzel, Katrin, Ekaterina Lapshinova-Koltunski & Kerstin Anna Kunz (eds.). New perspectives on cohesion and coherence: Implications for translation.
7. Hansen-Schirra, Silvia, Oliver Czulo & Sascha Hofmann (eds). Empirical modelling of translation and interpreting.
8. Svoboda, Tomáš, Łucja Biel & Krzysztof Łoboda (eds.). Quality aspects in institutional translation.
9. Fox, Wendy. Can integrated titles improve the viewing experience? Investigating the impact of subtitling on the reception and enjoyment of film using eye tracking and questionnaire data.
10. Moran, Steven & Michael Cysouw. The Unicode cookbook for linguists: Managing writing systems using orthography profiles

ISSN: 2364-8899

Preface

This text is meant as a practical guide for linguists and programmers who work with data in multilingual computational environments. We introduce the basic concepts needed to understand how writing systems and character encodings function, and how they work together.

The intersection of the Unicode Standard and the International Phonetic Alphabet is often met with frustration by users. Nevertheless, the two standards have provided language researchers with the computational architecture needed to process, publish and analyze data from many different languages. We bring to light common, but not always transparent, pitfalls that researchers face when working with Unicode and IPA.

In our research, we use quantitative methods to compare languages to uncover and clarify their phylogenetic relationships. However, the majority of lexical data available from the world's languages is in author- or document-specific orthographies. Having identified and overcome the pitfalls involved in making writing systems and character encodings syntactically and semantically interoperable (to the extent that they can be), we have created a suite of open-source Python and R software packages to work with languages using profiles that adequately describe their orthographic conventions. Using these tools in combination with orthography profiles allows users to tokenize and transliterate text from diverse sources, so that they can be meaningfully compared and analyzed.

We welcome comments and corrections regarding this book, our source code, and the supplemental case studies that we provide online.[1] Please use the issue tracker, email us directly, or make suggestions on PaperHive.[2]

Steven Moran
Michael Cysouw

[1] https://github.com/unicode-cookbook/

[2] https://paperhive.org/

Acknowledgments

We gratefully acknowledge Robert Forkel, Jeff Good, Jeremy Kahn, Dan McCloy, Sebastian Nordhoff, and Richard Wright, for insights and inspiration. The research leading to these results has received funding from the European Research Council under the European Union's Seventh Framework Programme (FP7/2007-2013)/ERC grant agreement n° 240816 (PI Michael Cysouw).

Contents

1 Writing systems

1.1 Introduction

Writing systems arise and develop in a complex mixture of cultural, technological and practical pressures. They tend to be highly conservative, in that people who have learned to read and write in a specific way – however impractical or tedious – are mostly unwilling to change their habits. Writers tend to resist spelling reforms. In all literate societies there exists a strong socio-political mainstream that tries to force unification of writing (for example by strongly enforcing "right" from "wrong" spelling in schools). However, there are also communities of users who take as many liberties in their writing as they can get away with.

For example, the writing of tone diacritics in Yoruba is often proclaimed to be the right way to write, although many users of Yoruba orthography seem to be perfectly fine with leaving them out. As pointed out by the proponents of the official rules, there are some homographs when leaving out the tone diacritics (Olúmúyìw 2013: 44). However, writing systems (and the languages they represent) are normally full of homographs (and homophones), which is not a problem at all for speakers of the language. More importantly, writing is not just a purely functional tool, but just as importantly it is a mechanism to signal social affiliation. By showing that you *know the rules* of expressing yourself in writing, others will more easily accept you as a worthy participant in their group – whether it means following the official rules when writing a job application or conforming to the informal rules when writing text messages. The case of Yoruba writing is an exemplary case, as even after more than a century of efforts to standardize the writing systems, there is still a wide range of variation of writing in daily use (Olúmúyìw 2013).

Formalizing orthographic structure

The resulting cumbersome and often illogical structure of writing systems, and the enormous variability of existing writing systems for the world's languages, is a fact of life that scholars have to accept and they should try to adapt to as well as they can. Our goal in this book is a proposal for how to do exactly that:

formalize knowledge about individual writing systems in a form that is easy to use for linguists in daily practice, and at the same time computer-readable for automated processing.

When considering worldwide linguistic diversity, including the many lesser-studied and endangered languages, there exist numerous different orthographies using symbols from the same scripts. For example, there are hundreds of orthographies using Latin-based alphabetic scripts. All of these orthographies use the same symbols, but these symbols differ in meaning and usage throughout the various orthographies. To be able to computationally use and compare different orthographies, we need a way to specify all orthographic idiosyncrasies in a computer-readable format. We call such specifications ORTHOGRAPHY PROFILES. Ideally, these specifications have to be integrated into so-called Unicode Locales,[1] though we will argue that in practice this is often not the most useful solution for the kind of problems arising in the daily practice of many linguists. Consequently, a central goal of this book is to flesh out the linguistic-specific challenges regarding Unicode Locales and to work out suggestions to simplify their structure for usage in a linguistic context. Conversely, we also aim to improve linguists' understanding and appreciation for the accomplishments of the Unicode Consortium in the development of the Unicode Standard.

The need to use computational methods to compare different orthographies arises most forcefully in the context of language comparison. Concretely, the proper processing of orthographies and transcription systems becomes critical for the development of quantitative methods for language comparison and historical reconstruction. In order to investigate worldwide linguistic variation and to model the historical and areal processes that underlie linguistic diversity, it is crucial that we are able to flexibly process numerous resources in different orthographies. In many cases even different resources on the same language use different orthographic conventions. Another orthographic challenge that we encounter regularly in our linguistic practice is electronic resources on a particular language that claim to follow a specific orthographic convention (often a resource-specific convention), but on closer inspection such resources are almost always not consistently encoded. Thus, a second goal of our orthography profiles is to allow for an easy specification of orthographic conventions, and use such profiles to check consistency and to report errors to be corrected.

A central step in our proposed solution to this problem is the tailored grapheme separation of strings of symbols, a process we call GRAPHEME TOKENIZATION. Basically, given some strings of symbols (e.g. morphemes, words, sentences) in

[1]http://cldr.unicode.org/locale_faq-html

a specific source, our first processing step is to specify how these strings should be separated into graphemes, considering the specific orthographic conventions used in a particular source document. Our experience is that such a graphemic tokenization can often be performed reasonably accurately without extensive in-depth knowledge about the phonetic and phonological details of the language in question. For example, the specification that <ou> is a grapheme of English is a much easier task than to specify what exactly the phonetic values of this grapheme are in any specific occurrence in English words. Grapheme separation is a task that can be performed relatively reliably and with limited time and resources (compare, for example, the daunting task of creating a complete phonetic or phonological normalization).

Although grapheme tokenization is only one part of the solution, it is an important and highly fruitful processing step. Given a grapheme tokenization, various subsequent tasks become easier, for instance (a) temporarily reducing the orthography in a processing pipeline, e.g. only distinguishing high versus low vowels; (b) normalizing orthographies across sources (often including temporary reduction of oppositions), e.g. specifying an (approximate) mapping to the International Phonetic Alphabet; (c) using co-occurrence statistics across different languages (or different sources in the same language) to estimate the probability of grapheme matches, e.g. with the goal to find regular sound changes between related languages or transliterations between different sources in the same language.

Structure of this book

Before we deal with these proposals we will first discuss the theoretical background on text encoding, on the Unicode Standard, and on the International Phonetic Alphabet. In the remainder of this chapter, we give an extended introduction to the notion of encoding (Section 1.2) and the principles of writing systems from a linguistic perspective (Section 1.3). In Chapter 2, we discuss the notions of encoding and writing systems from the perspective of the Unicode Consortium. We consider the Unicode Standard to be a breakthrough (and ongoing) development that fundamentally changed the way we look at writing systems, and we aim to provide here a slightly more in-depth survey of the many techniques that are available in the standard. A good appreciation for the solutions that the Unicode Consortium has created allows for a thorough understanding of the possible pitfalls that one might encounter when using the Unicode Standard in general (Chapter 3). Linguists are more often interested in using the Unicode Standard with the International Phonetic Alphabet (IPA). We first provide a history of the development of the IPA and early attempts to encode it electronically (Chapter 4) before we discuss the rather problematic marriage of the IPA with the Unicode Standard (Chapter 5).

In the second part of the book (Chapters 6, 7 & 8) we describe our proposals of how to deal with the Unicode Standard in the daily practice of (comparative) linguistics. First, we provide some practical recommendations for using the Unicode Standard and IPA for ordinary working linguists and for computer programmers (Chapter 6). Second, we discuss the challenges of characterizing a writing system; to solve these problems, we propose the notions of orthography profiles, closely related to Unicode locale descriptions (Chapter 7). Lastly, we provide an introduction to two open source libraries that we have developed, in Python and R, for working with linguistic data and orthography profiles (Chapter 8).

Conventions

The following conventions are adhered to in this book. All phonemic and phonetic representations are given in the International Phonetic Alphabet (IPA), unless noted otherwise (The International Phonetic Association 2015). Standard conventions are used for distinguishing between graphemic < >, phonemic / / and phonetic [ ] representations. For character descriptions, we follow the notational conventions of the Unicode Standard (The Unicode Consortium 2018). Character names are represented in small capital letters (e.g. LATIN SMALL LETTER SCHWA) and code points are expressed as U+*n*, where *n* is a four to six digit hexadecimal number, e.g. U+0256, which can be rendered as the glyph <ə>.

1.2 Encoding

There are many in-depth histories of the origin and development of writing systems (e.g. Robinson 1995; Powell 2012), a story that we therefore will not repeat here. However, the history of turning writing into machine-readable code is not so often told, so we decided to offer a short survey of the major developments of such encoding here.[2] This history turns out to be intimately related to the history of telegraphic communication.

[2]Because of the recent history as summarized in this section, we have used mostly rather ephemeral internet sources. When not referenced by traditional literature in the bibliography, we have used http://www.unicode.org/history/ and various Wikipedia pages for the information presented here. A useful survey of the historical development of the physical hardware of telegraphy and telecommunication is Huurdeman (2003). Most books that discuss the development of encoding of telegraphic communication focus of cryptography, e.g. Singh (1999),

Telegraphy

Writing systems have existed for roughly 6000 years, allowing people to exchange messages through time and space. Additionally, to quickly bridge large geographic distances, telegraphic systems of communication (from Greek *τῆλε γράφειν* 'distant writing') have a long and widespread history since ancient times. The most common telegraphic systems worldwide are so-called whistled languages (Meyer 2015), but also drumming languages (Meyer et al. 2012) and signaling by smoke, fire, flags, or even changes in water levels through hydraulic pressure have been used as forms of telegraphy.

Telegraphy was reinvigorated at the end of the eighteenth century through the introduction of so-called semaphoric systems by Claude Chapelle to convey messages over large distances. Originally, various specially designed contraptions were used to send messages. Today, descendants of these systems are still in limited use, for example utilizing flags or flashing lights. The innovation of those semaphoric systems was that all characters of the written language were replaced one-to-one by visual signals. Since then, all telegraphic systems have adopted this principle,[3] namely that any language to be transmitted first has to be turned into some orthographic system, which subsequently is encoded for transmission by the sender, and then turned back into orthographic representation at the receiver side. This of course implies that the usefulness of any such telegraphic encoding completely depends on the sometimes rather haphazard structure of orthographic systems.

In the nineteenth century, electric telegraphy led to a further innovation in which written language characters were encoded by signals sent through a copper wire. Originally, BISIGNAL CODES were used, consisting of two different signals. For example, Carl Friedrich Gauss in 1833 used positive and negative current (Mania 2008: 282). More famous and influential, Samuel Morse in 1836 used long and short pulses. In those bisignal codes each character from the written language was encoded with a different number of signals (between one and five), so two different separators are needed: one between signals and one between characters. For example, in Morse-code there is a short pause between signals and a long pause between characters.[4]

and forego the rather interesting story of open, i.e. non-cryptographic, encoding that is related here.

[3] Sound- and video-based telecommunication take a different approach by ignoring the written version of language and they directly encode sound waves or light patterns.

[4] Actually, Morse-code also includes an extra long pause between words. Interestingly, it took a long time to consider the written word boundary – using white-space – as a bona-fide character

Binary encoding

From those bisignal encodings, true binary codes developed with a fixed length of signals per character. In such systems only a single separator between signals is needed, because the separation between characters can be established by counting until a fixed number of signals has passed.[5] In the context of electric telegraphy, such a binary code system was first established by Émile Baudot in 1870, using a fixed combination of five signals for each written character.[6] There are $2^5 = 32$ possible combinations when using five binary signals; an encoding today designated as 5-bit. These codes are sufficient for all Latin letters, but of course they do not suffice for all written symbols, including punctuation and digits. As a solution, the Baudot code uses a so-called shift character, which signifies that from that point onwards – until shifted back – a different encoding is used, allowing for yet another set of 32 codes. In effect, this means that the Baudot code, and the International Telegraph Alphabet (ITA) derived from it, had an extra bit of information, so the encoding is actually 6-bit (with $2^6 = 64$ different possible characters). For decades, this encoding was the standard for all telegraphy and it is still in limited use today.

To also allow for different uppercase and lowercase letters and for a large variety of control characters to be used in the newly developing technology of computers, the American Standards Association decided to propose a new 7-bit encoding in 1963 (with $2^7 = 128$ different possible characters), known as the American Standard Code for Information Interchange (ASCII), geared towards the encoding of English orthography. With the ascent of other orthographies in computer usage, the wish to encode further variations of Latin letters (including German <ß> and various letters with diacritics, e.g. <è>) led the Digital Equipment Corporation to introduce an 8-bit Multinational Character Set (MCS, with $2^8 = 256$ different possible characters), first used with the introduction of the VT220 Terminal in 1983.

that should simply be encoded with its own code point. This happened only with the revision of the Baudot-code (see below) by Donald Murray in 1901, in which he introduced a specific white-space code. This principle has been followed ever since.

[5] Of course, no explicit separator is needed at all when the timing of the signals is known, which is the principle used in all modern telecommunication systems. An important modern consideration is also how to know where to start counting when you did not catch the start of a message, something that is known in Unicode as self synchronization.

[6] True binary codes have a longer history, going back at least to the Baconian cipher devised by Francis Bacon in 1605. However, the proposal by Baudot was the quintessential proposal leading to all modern systems.

Because 256 characters were clearly not enough for the unique representation of many different characters needed in the world's writing systems, the ISO/IEC 8859 standard in 1987 extended the MCS to include 16 different 8-bit code pages. For example, part 5 was used for Cyrillic characters, part 6 for Arabic, and part 7 for Greek. This system was almost immediately understood to be insufficient and impractical, so various initiatives to extend and reorganize the encoding started in the 1980s. This led, for example, to various proprietary encodings from Microsoft (e.g. Windows Latin 1) and Apple (e.g. Mac OS Roman), which one still sometimes encounters today.

In the 1980s various people started to develop true international code sets. In the United States, a group of computer scientists formed the UNICODE CONSORTIUM, proposing a 16-bit encoding in 1991 (with $2^{16} = 65,536$ different possible characters). At the same time in Europe, the INTERNATIONAL ORGANIZATION FOR STANDARDIZATION (ISO) was working on ISO 10646 to replace the ISO/IEC 8859 standard. Their first draft of the UNIVERSAL CHARACTER SET (UCS) in 1990 was 31-bit (with theoretically $2^{31} = 2,147,483,648$ possible characters, but because of some technical restrictions only 679,477,248 were allowed). Since 1991, the Unicode Consortium and the ISO jointly develop the UNICODE STANDARD, or ISO/IEC 10646, leading to the current system including the original 16-bit Unicode proposal as the BASIC MULTILINGUAL PLANE, and 16 additional planes of 16-bit for further extensions (with in total $(1 + 16)\ 2^{16} = 1,114,112$ possible characters). The most recent version of the Unicode Standard (currently at version number 11.0.0) was published in June 2018 and it defines 137,374 different characters (The Unicode Consortium 2018).

In the next section we provide a very brief overview of the linguistic terminology concerning writing systems before turning to the slightly different computational terminology in the subsequent chapter on the Unicode Standard.

1.3 Linguistic terminology

Linguistically speaking, a WRITING SYSTEM is a symbolic system that uses visible or tactile signs to represent language in a systematic way. The term writing system has two mutually exclusive meanings. First, it may refer to the way a particular language is written. In this sense the term refers to the writing system of a particular language, as, for example, in *the Serbian writing system uses two scripts: Latin and Cyrillic.* Second, the term writing system may also refer to a type of symbolic system as, for example, in *alphabetic writing system.* In this latter sense the term refers to how scripts have been classified according to the way that they encode language, as in, for example, *the Latin and Cyrillic scripts are both alphabetic writing systems.* To avoid confusion, this second notion of writing system would more aptly have been called SCRIPT SYSTEM.

Writing systems

Focusing on the first sense of WRITING SYSTEM described above, we distinguish between two different kinds of writing systems used for a particular language, namely transcriptions and orthographies. First, TRANSCRIPTION is a scientific procedure (and also the result of that procedure) for graphically representing the sounds of human speech at the phonetic level. It incorporates a set of unambiguous symbols to represent speech sounds, including conventions that specify how these symbols should be combined. A transcription system is a specific system of symbols and rules used for transcription of the sounds of a spoken language variety. In principle, a transcription system should be language-independent, in that it should be applicable to all spoken human languages. The INTERNATIONAL PHONETIC ALPHABET (IPA) is a commonly used transcription system that provides a medium for transcribing languages at the phonetic level. However, there is a long history of alternative kinds of transcription systems (see Kemp 2006) and today various alternatives are in widespread use (e.g. X-SAMPA and Cyrillic-based phonetic transcription systems). Many users of IPA do not follow the standard to the letter, and many dialects based on the IPA have emerged, e.g. the Africanist and Americanist transcription systems. Note that IPA symbols are also often used to represent language on a phonemic level. It is important to realize that in this usage the IPA symbols are not a transcription system, but rather an orthography (though with strong links to the pronunciation). Further, a transcription system does not need to be as highly detailed as the IPA. It can also be a system of broad sound classes. Although such an approximative transcription is not normally used in linguistics, it is widespread in technological approaches (Soundex and variants, e.g. Knuth 1973: 391–392; Postel 1969; Beider & Morse 2008), and it is sometimes fruitfully used in automatic approaches to historical linguistics (Dolgopolsky 1986; List 2012; Brown et al. 2013).

Second, an ORTHOGRAPHY specifies the symbols, punctuations, and the rules in which a specific language is written in a standardized way. Orthographies are often based on a phonemic analysis, but they almost always include idiosyncrasies because of historical developments (like sound changes or loans) and because of the widely-followed principle of lexical integrity (i.e. the attempt to write the same lexical root in a consistent way, also when synchronic phonemic rules change the pronunciation, as for example with final devoicing in many Germanic languages). Orthographies are language-specific (and often even resource-specific), although individual symbols or rules might be shared between languages. A PRACTICAL ORTHOGRAPHY is a strongly phoneme-based writing system designed for practical use by speakers. The mapping relation between phonemes and graphemes in practical orthographies is purposely shallow, i.e. there is mostly a systematic and faithful mapping from a phoneme to a grapheme. Practical orthographies are intended to jumpstart written materials development by correlating a writing system with the sound units of a language (Meinhof & Jones 1928). Symbols from the IPA are often used by linguists in the development of such practical orthographies for languages without writing systems, though this usage of IPA symbols should not be confused with transcription (as defined above).

Further, a TRANSLITERATION is a mapping between two different orthographies. It is the process of "recording the graphic symbols of one writing system in terms of the corresponding graphic symbols of a second writing system" (Kemp 2006: 396). In straightforward cases, such a transliteration is simply a matter of replacing one symbol with another. However, there are widespread complications, like one-to-many or many-to-many mappings, which are not always easy, or even possible, to solve without listing all cases individually (cf. Moran 2012: Ch. 2).

Script systems

Different kinds of writing systems are classified into script systems. A SCRIPT is a collection of distinct symbols as employed by one or more orthographies. For example, both Serbian and Russian are written with subsets of the Cyrillic script. A single language, like Serbian or Japanese, can also be written using orthographies based on different scripts. Over the years linguists have classified script systems in a variety of ways, with the tripartite classification of logographic, syllabic, and alphabetic remaining the most popular, even though there are at least half a dozen different types of script systems that can be distinguished (Daniels 1990; 1996).

Breaking it down further, a script consists of GRAPHEMES, which are writing system-specific minimally distinctive symbols (see below). Graphemes may consist of one or more CHARACTERS. The term CHARACTER is overladen. In the linguistic terminology of writing systems, a CHARACTER is a general term for any self-contained element in a writing system. A second interpretation is used as a conventional term for a unit in the Chinese writing system (Daniels 1996). In technical terminology, a CHARACTER refers to the electronic encoding of a component in a writing system that has semantic value (see Section 2.3). Thus in this work we must navigate between the general linguistic and technical terms for CHARACTER and GRAPHEME because of how these notions are defined and how they relate at the intersection between the International Phonetic Alphabet and the Unicode Standard (Chapter 5).

Although in literate societies most people have a strong intuition about what the characters are in their particular orthography or orthographies, it turns out that the separation of an orthography into separate characters is far from trivial. The widespread intuitive notion of a character is strongly biased towards educational traditions, like the alphabet taught at schools, and technological possibilities, like the available type pieces in a printer's job case, the keys on a typewriter, or the symbols displayed in Microsoft Word's symbol browser. In practice, characters often consist of multiple building blocks, each of which could be considered a character in its own right. For example, although a Chinese character may be considered to be a single basic unanalyzable unit, at a more fine-grained level of analysis the internal structure of Chinese characters is often comprised of smaller semantic and phonetic units that should be considered characters (Sproat 2000). In alphabetic scripts, this problem is most forcefully exemplified by diacritics.

A DIACRITIC is a mark, or series of marks, that may be above, below, before, after, through, around, or between other characters (Gaultney 2002). Diacritics are sometimes used to distinguish homophonous words, but they are more often used to indicate a modified pronunciation (Daniels & Bright 1996: xli). The central question is whether, for example, <e>, <è>, <a> and <à> should be considered four characters, or different combinations of three characters, i.e. <a>, <e>, and <◌̀>. In general, multiple characters together can form another character, and it is not always possible to decide on principled grounds what should be the basic building blocks of an orthography.

For that reason, it is better to analyze an orthography as a collection of graphemes. A GRAPHEME is the basic, minimally distinctive symbol of a particular writing system. It was modeled after the term PHONEME (an abstract representation of a distinct sound in a specific language) and as such it represents a contrastive graphical unit in a writing system (see Kohrt 1986 for a historical overview of the term GRAPHEME). Most importantly, a single grapheme regularly consists of multiple characters, like <th>, <ou> and <gh> in English (note that each character in these graphemes is also a separate grapheme in English). Such complex graphemes are often used to represent single phonemes. So, a combination of characters is used to represent a single phoneme. Note that the opposite is also found in writing systems, in cases in which a single character represents a combination of two or more phonemes. For example, <x> in English orthography sometimes represents a combination of the phonemes /k/ and /s/, as in the word 'index' [ˈɪnˌdɛks]; other times it is pronounced as /z/, such as in the words 'Xerox' [ˈzɪrˌɑks]; and in 'example' [ɪgˈzæmpəl] it is a combination of /g/ and /s/. As one can see, there can be non-trivial mappings between graphemes and phonemes in orthographies like English, e.g. 'give', 'gin', 'jingle', where the graphemes <g> and <j> and the phonemes /g/ and /dʒ/ have a complex mapping.

Further, conditioned or free variants of a grapheme are called ALLOGRAPHS. For example, the distinctive forms of Greek sigma are conditioned, with <σ> being used word-internally and <ς> being used at the end of a word. In sum, there are many-to-many relationships between phonemes and graphemes as they are expressed in the myriad of language- and resource-specific orthographies.

Summary

This exposition of the linguistic terminology involved in describing writing systems has been purposely brief. We have highlighted some of the linguistic notions that are pertinent to, yet sometimes confused with, the technical definitions developed for the computational processing of the world's writing systems, which we describe in the next Chapter.

2 The Unicode approach

2.1 Background

The conceptualization and terminology of writing systems was rejuvenated by the development of the Unicode Standard, with major input from Mark Davis, co-founder and long-term president of the Unicode Consortium. For many years, "exotic" writing systems and phonetic transcription systems on personal computers were constrained by the American Standard Code for Information Interchange (ASCII) character encoding scheme, based on the Latin script, which only allowed for a strongly limited number of different symbols to be encoded. This implied that users could either use and adopt the (extended) Latin alphabet or they could assign new symbols to the small number of code points in the ASCII encoding scheme to be rendered by a specifically designed font (Bird & Simons 2003). In this situation, it was necessary to specify the font together with each document to ensure the rightful display of its content. To alleviate this problem of assigning different symbols to the same code points, in the late 80s and early 90s the Unicode Consortium set itself the ambitious goal of developing a single universal character encoding to provide a unique number, a code point, for every character in the world's writing systems. Nowadays, the Unicode Standard is the default encoding of the technologies that support the World Wide Web and for all modern operating systems, software and programming languages.

2.2 The Unicode Standard

The Unicode Standard represents a massive step forward because it aims to eradicate the distinction between universal (ASCII) versus language-particular (font) by adding as much language-specific information as possible into the universal standard. However, there are still language/resource-specific specifications necessary for the proper usage of Unicode, as will be discussed below. Within the Unicode structure many of these specifications can be captured by so-called Unicode Locales, so we are moving to a new distinction of universal (Unicode Standard) versus language-particular (Unicode Locale). The major gain is much larger compatibility on the universal level (because Unicode standardizes a much greater portion of writing system diversity), and much better possibilities for automated processing on the language-particular level (because Unicode Locales are machine-readable specifications).

Each version of the Unicode Standard (The Unicode Consortium 2018, as of writing at version 11.0.0) consists of a set of specifications and guidelines that include (i) a core specification, (ii) code charts, (iii) standard annexes and (iv) a character database.[1] The CORE SPECIFICATION is a book aimed at human readers that describes the formal standard for encoding multilingual text. The CODE CHARTS provide a human-readable online reference to the character contents of the Unicode Standard in the form of PDF files. The UNICODE STANDARD ANNEXES (UAX) are a set of technical standards that describe the implementation of the Unicode Standard for software development, web standards, and programming languages. The UNICODE CHARACTER DATABASE (UCD) is a set of computer-readable text files that describe the character properties, including a set of rich character and writing system semantics, for each character in the Unicode Standard. In this section, we introduce the basic Unicode concepts, but we will leave out many details. Please consult the above-mentioned full documentation for a more detailed discussion. Further note that the Unicode Standard is exactly that, namely a standard. It normatively describes notions and rules to be followed. In the actual practice of applying this standard in a computational setting, a specific implementation is necessary. The most widely used implementation of the Unicode Standard is the INTERNATIONAL COMPONENTS FOR UNICODE (ICU), which offers C/C++ and Java libraries implementing the Unicode Standard.[2]

2.3 Character encoding system

The Unicode Standard is a CHARACTER ENCODING SYSTEM whose goal is to support the interchange and processing of written characters and text in a computational

[1] All documents of the Unicode Standard are available at: http://www.unicode.org/versions/latest/. For a quick survey of the use of terminology inside the Unicode Standard, their glossary is particularly useful, available at: http://www.unicode.org/glossary/. For a general introduction to the principles of Unicode, Chapter 2 of the core specification, called GENERAL STRUCTURE, is particularly insightful. Unlike many other documents in the Unicode Standard, this general introduction is relatively easy to read and illustrated with many interesting examples from various orthographic traditions from all over the world.

[2] More information about the ICU is available here: http://icu-project.org.

setting.[3] Underlyingly, the character encoding is represented by a range of numerical values called a CODE SPACE, which is used to encode a set of characters. A CODE POINT is a unique non-negative integer within a code space (i.e. within a certain numerical range). In the Unicode Standard character encoding system, an ABSTRACT CHARACTER, for example the LATIN SMALL LETTER P, is mapped to a particular code point, in this case the decimal value 112, normally represented in hexadecimal, which then looks in Unicode parlance as U+0070. That encoded abstract character is rendered on a computer screen (or printed page) as a GLYPH, e.g. <p>, depending on the FONT and the context in which that character appears.

In Unicode Standard terminology, an (abstract) CHARACTER is the basic encoding unit. The term CHARACTER can be quite confusing due to its alternative definitions across different scientific disciplines and because in general the word CHARACTER means many different things to different people. It is therefore often preferable to refer to Unicode characters simply as CODE POINTS, because there is a one-to-one mapping between Unicode characters and their numeric representation. In the Unicode approach, a character refers to the abstract meaning and/or general shape, rather than a specific shape, though in code tables some form of visual representation is essential for the reader's understanding. Unicode defines characters as abstractions of orthographic symbols, and it does not define visualizations for these characters (although it does present examples). In contrast, a GLYPH is a concrete graphical representation of a character as it appears when rendered (or rasterized) and displayed on an electronic device or on printed paper. For example, <g g g g g **g**> are different glyphs of the same character, i.e. they may be rendered differently depending on the typography being used, but they all share the same code point. From the perspective of Unicode they are *the same thing*. In this approach, a FONT is then simply a collection of glyphs connected to code points. Allography is not specified in Unicode (barring a few exceptional cases, due to legacy encoding issues), but can be specified in a font as a CONTEXTUAL VARIANT (aka presentation form).

Each code point in the Unicode Standard is associated with a set of CHARACTER PROPERTIES as defined by the Unicode character property model.[4] Basically, those

[3] An insightful reviewer notes that the term ENCODING is used for both sequences of code points and text encoded as bit patterns. Hence a Unicode-aware programmer might prefer to say that UTF-8, UTF-16, etc., are Unicode encoding systems. The issue is that the Unicode Standard introduces a layer of indirection between characters and bit patterns, i.e. the code point, which can be encoded differently by different encoding systems.

[4] The character property model is described in http://www.unicode.org/reports/tr23/, but the actual properties are described in http://www.unicode.org/reports/tr44/. A simplified overview of the properties is available at: http://userguide.icu-project.org/strings/properties. The ac-

properties are just a long list of values for each character. For example, code point U+0047 has the following properties (among many others):

- Name: LATIN CAPITAL LETTER G
- Alphabetic: YES
- Uppercase: YES
- Script: LATIN
- Extender: NO
- Simple_Lowercase_Mapping: 0067

These properties contain the basic information of the Unicode Standard and they are necessary to define the correct behavior and conformance required for interoperability in and across different software implementations (as defined in the Unicode Standard Annexes). The character properties assigned to each code point are based on each character's behavior in real-world writing traditions. For example, the corresponding lowercase character to U+0047 is U+0067.[5] Another use of properties is to define the script of a character.[6] In practice, script is simply defined for each character as the explicit SCRIPT property in the Unicode Character Database.

One frequently referenced property is the BLOCK property, which is often used in software applications to impose some structure on the large number of Unicode characters. Each character in Unicode belongs to a specific block. These blocks are basically an organizational structure to alleviate the administrative burden of keeping Unicode up-to-date. Blocks consist of characters that in some way belong together, so that characters are easier to find. Some blocks are connected with a specific script, like the Hebrew block or the Gujarati block. However, blocks are predefined ranges of code points, and often there will come a point after which the range is completely filled. Any extra characters will have to be assigned somewhere else. There is, for example, a block ARABIC, which contains most Arabic symbols. However, there is also a block ARABIC SUPPLEMENT, ARABIC PRESENTATION FORMS-A and ARABIC PRESENTATION FORMS-B. The situation with Latin symbols is even more extreme. In general, the names of blocks

tual code tables listing all properties for all Unicode code points are available at: http://www.unicode.org/Public/UCD/latest/ucd/.

[5] Note that the relation between uppercase and lowercase is in many situations much more complex than this, and Unicode has further specifications for those cases.

[6] The Glossary of Unicode Terms defines the term SCRIPT as a "collection of letters and other written signs used to represent textual information in one or more writing systems. For example, Russian is written with a subset of the Cyrillic script; Ukrainian is written with a different subset. The Japanese writing system uses several scripts."

should not be taken as a definitional statement. For example, many IPA symbols are not located in the aptly-named block IPA EXTENSIONS, but in other blocks (see Section 5.2).

2.4 Grapheme clusters

There are many cases in which a sequence of characters (i.e. a sequence of more than one code point) represents what a user perceives as an individual unit in a particular orthographic writing system. For this reason the Unicode Standard differentiates between ABSTRACT CHARACTER and USER-PERCEIVED CHARACTER. Sequences of multiple code points that correspond to a single user-perceived characters are called GRAPHEME CLUSTERS in Unicode parlance. Grapheme clusters come in two flavors: (default) grapheme clusters and tailored grapheme clusters.

The (default) GRAPHEME CLUSTERS are locale-independent graphemes, i.e. they always apply when a particular combination of characters occurs independent of the writing system in which they are used. These character combinations are defined in the Unicode Standard as functioning as one TEXT ELEMENT.[7] The simplest example of a grapheme cluster is a base character followed by a letter modifier character. For example, the sequence <n> + <◌̃> (i.e. LATIN SMALL LETTER N at U+006E, followed by COMBINING TILDE at U+0303) combines visually into <ñ>, a user-perceived character in writing systems like that of Spanish. In effect, what the user perceives as a single character actually involves a multi-code-point sequence. Note that this specific sequence can also be represented with a single so-called PRECOMPOSED CODE POINT, the LATIN SMALL LETTER N WITH TILDE at U+00F1, but this is not the case for all multi-code-point character sequences. A solution to the problem of multiple encodings for the same text element was developed early on in the Unicode Standard. It is called CANONICAL EQUIVALENCE, e.g. for <ñ>, the sequence U+006E U+0303 should in all situations be treated identically to the precomposed U+00F1. By doing so, Unicode can also support special or precomposed characters in legacy character sets. To determine canonical equivalence, the Unicode Standard offers different kinds of normalization to either decompose precomposed characters (called NFD for NORMALIZATION FORM CANONICAL DECOMPOSITION) or to combine sequences of code points into precomposed characters (called NFC for NORMALIZATION FORM CANONICAL COMPO-

[7] The Glossary of Unicode Terms defines TEXT ELEMENT as: "A minimum unit of text in relation to a particular text process, in the context of a given writing system. In general, the mapping between text elements and code points is many-to-many."

sition).[8] In current software development practice, NFC seems to be preferred in most situations and is widely proposed as the preferred canonical form. We discuss Unicode normalization in detail in Section 3.9.

More difficult for text processing, because less standardized, is what the Unicode Standard terms tailored grapheme clusters.[9] Tailored grapheme clusters are locale-dependent graphemes, i.e. such combination of characters do not function as text elements in all situations. Examples include the sequence <c> + <h> for the Slovak digraph <ch> and the sequence <ky> in the Sisaala practical orthography, which is pronounced as IPA /tʃ/ (Moran 2006). These grapheme clusters are tailored in the sense that they must be specified on a language-by-language or writing-system-by-writing-system basis. They are also grapheme clusters in these orthographies for processes such as collation (i.e. sorting).[10]

The Unicode Standard provides technical specifications for creating locale specific data in so-called Unicode Locales, i.e. specifications that define a set of language-specific elements (e.g. tailored grapheme clusters, collation order, capitalization equivalence), as well as other special information, like how to format numbers, dates, or currencies. Locale descriptions are saved in the Common Locale Data Repository (CLDR),[11] a repository of language-specific definitions of writing system properties, each of which describes specific usages of characters. Each locale can be encoded in a document using the Locale Data Markup Language (LDML). LDML is an XML format and vocabulary for the exchange of structured locale data. Unicode Locale Descriptions allow users to define language- or even resource-specific writing systems or orthographies.[12] However, Unicode Locales have various drawbacks for the daily practice of scientific linguistic research in a multilingual setting.

[8]See the Unicode Standard Annex #15, Unicode Normalization Forms (http://unicode.org/reports/tr15/), which provides a detailed description of normalization algorithms and illustrated examples.

[9]http://unicode.org/reports/tr29/

[10]https://www.unicode.org/glossary/#collation

[11]More information about the CLDR can be found here: http://cldr.unicode.org/.

[12]The Glossary of Unicode Terms defines writing system only very loosely, as it is not a central concept in the Unicode Standard. A writing system is, "A set of rules for using one or more scripts to write a particular language. Examples include the American English writing system, the British English writing system, the French writing system, and the Japanese writing system."

3 Unicode pitfalls

3.1 Wrong it ain't

In this chapter we describe some of the most common pitfalls that we have encountered when using the Unicode Standard in our own work, or in discussion with other linguists. This section is not meant as a criticism of the decisions made by the Unicode Consortium; rather we aim to highlight where the technical aspects of the Unicode Standard diverge from many users' intuitions. What have sometimes been referred to as problems or inconsistencies in the Unicode Standard are mostly due to legacy compatibility issues, which can lead to unexpected behavior by linguists using the standard. However, there are also some cases in which the Unicode Standard has made decisions that theoretically could have been made differently, but for some reason or another (mostly very good reasons) were accepted as they are now. We call such behavior that executes without error but does something different than the user expected – often unknowingly – a PITFALL.

In this context, it is important to realize that the Unicode Standard was not developed to solve linguistic problems per se, but to offer a consistent computational environment for written language. In those cases in which the Unicode Standard behaves differently than expected, we think it is important not to dismiss Unicode as wrong or deficient, because our experience is that in almost all cases the behavior of the Unicode Standard has been particularly well thought through. The Unicode Consortium has a wide-ranging view of matters and often examines important practical use cases that are not normally considered from a linguistic point of view. Our general guideline for dealing with the Unicode Standard is to accept it as it is, and not to tilt at windmills. Alternatively, of course, it is possible to actively engage in the development of the standard itself, an effort that is highly appreciated by the Unicode Consortium.

3.2 Pitfall: Characters are not glyphs

A central principle of Unicode is the distinction between character and glyph. A character is the abstract notion of a symbol in a writing system, while a glyph is the visual representation of such a symbol. In practice, there is a complex interaction between characters and glyphs. A single Unicode character may of course be rendered as a single glyph. However, a character may also be a piece of a glyph, or vice-versa. Actually, all possible relations between glyphs and characters are attested.

First, a single character may have different contextually determined glyphs. For example, characters in writing systems like Hebrew and Arabic have different glyphs depending on where they appear in a word. Some letters in Hebrew change their form at the end of the word, and in Arabic, primary letters have four contextually-sensitive variants (isolated, word initial, medial and final).

Second, a single character may be rendered as a sequence of multiple glyphs. For example, in Tamil one Unicode character may result in a combination of a consonant and vowel, which are rendered as two adjacent glyphs by fonts that support Tamil, e.g. TAMIL LETTER AU at U+0B94 represents a single character <ஔ>, composed of two glyphs <ஓ> and <ள>. Perhaps confusingly, in the Unicode Standard there are also two individual characters, i.e. TAMIL LETTER OO at U+0B93 and U+0BA9 TAMIL LETTER NNNA, each of which is a glyph. Another example is Sinhala SINHALA VOWEL SIGN KOMBU DEKA at U+0DDB <◌ෛ>, which is visually two glyphs, each represented by SINHALA VOWEL SIGN KOMBUVA at U+0DD9 <◌ෙ>.

Third, a single glyph may be a combination of multiple characters. For example, the ligature <ﬁ>, a single glyph, is the result of two characters, <f> and <i>, that have undergone glyph substitution by font rendering (see also Section 3.5). Like contextually-determined glyphs, ligatures are (intended) artifacts of text processing instructions. Finally, a single glyph may be a part of a character, as exemplified by diacritics like the diaeresis <◌̈> in <ë>.

Further, the rendering of a glyph is dependent on the font being used. For example, the Unicode character LATIN SMALL LETTER G appears as <g> and <g> in the Linux Libertine and Courier fonts, respectively, because their typefaces are designed differently. Furthermore, the font face may change the visual appearance of a character, for example Times New Roman two-story <a> changes to a single-story glyph in italics *<a>*. This becomes a real problem for some phonetic typesetting (see Section 5.3).

In sum, character-to-glyph mappings are complex technical issues that the Unicode Consortium has had to address in the development of the Unicode Standard. However, they can can be utterly confusing for the lay user because visual rendering does not (necessarily) indicate logical encoding.

3.3 Pitfall: Characters are not graphemes

The Unicode Standard encodes characters. This becomes most clear with the notion of grapheme. From a linguistic point of view, graphemes are the basic building blocks of a writing system (see Section 1.3). It is extremely common for writing systems to use combinations of multiple symbols (or letters) as a single grapheme, such as <sch>, <th> or <ei>. There is no way to encode such complex graphemes using the Unicode Standard.

The Unicode Standard deals with complex graphemes only inasmuch as they consist of base characters with diacritics (see Section 5.9 for a discussion of the notion of diacritic). The Unicode Standard calls such combinations *grapheme clusters*. Complex graphemes consisting of multiple base characters, like <sch>, are called *tailored grapheme clusters* (see Chapter 2).

There are special Unicode characters that glue together characters into larger tailored grapheme clusters, specifically the ZERO WIDTH JOINER at U+200D and the COMBINING GRAPHEME JOINER at U+034F. However, these characters are confusingly named (cf. Section 3.7). Both code points actually do not join characters, but explicitly separate them. The zero-width joiner (ZWJ) can be used to solve special problems related to ordering (called *collation* in Unicode parlance). The combining grapheme joiner (CGJ) can be used to separate characters that are not supposed to form ligatures.

To solve the issue of tailored grapheme clusters, Unicode offers some assistance in the form of Unicode Locales.[1] However, in the practice of linguistic research, this is not a real solution. To address this issue, we propose to use orthography profiles (see Chapter 7). Basically, both orthography profiles and Unicode Locales offer a way to specify tailored grapheme clusters. For example, for English one could specify that <sh> is such a cluster. Consequently, this sequence of characters is then always interpreted as a complex grapheme. For cases in which this is not the right decision, like in the English word *mishap*, the ZERO WIDTH JOINER at U+200D has to be entered between <s> and <h>.

[1] http://cldr.unicode.org/locale_faq-html

3.4 Pitfall: Missing glyphs

The Unicode Standard is often praised (and deservedly so) for solving many of the perennial problems with the interchange and display of the world's writing systems. Nevertheless, a common complaint from users is that some symbols do not display correctly, i.e. *not at all* or from a *fall back font*, e.g. a rectangle <⊠>, question mark <?>, or the Unicode replacement character <�>. The user's computer does not have the fonts installed that map the desired glyphs to Unicode characters. Therefore the glyphs cannot be displayed. This is not the Unicode Standard's fault because it is a character encoding system and not a font. Computer-internally everything works as expected; any handling of Unicode code points works independently of how they are displayed on the screen. So although users might see alien faces on display, they should not fret because everything is still technically in order below the surface.

There are two obstacles regarding missing glyphs. One is practical: designing glyphs includes many different considerations and it is a time-consuming process, especially when done well. Traditional expectations of what specific characters should look like need to be taken into account when designing glyphs. Those expectations are often not well documented, and it is mostly up to the knowledge and expertise of the font designer to try and conform to them. Furthermore, the number of characters supported by Unicode is vast. Therefore, most designers produce fonts that only include glyphs for certain parts of the Unicode Standard.

The second obstacle is technical: the maximum number of glyphs that can be defined by the TrueType font standard and the OpenType specification (ISO/IEC 14496-22:2015) is 65,535. The current version of the Unicode Standard contains 137,374 characters. Thus, no single font can provide individual glyphs for all Unicode characters.

A simple solution to missing glyphs is to install additional fonts providing additional glyphs. For broad coverage, there is the Noto font family, a project developed by Google, which covers over 100 scripts and nearly 64,000 characters.[2] The Unicode Consortium also provides, but does not endorse, an extensive list of fonts and font libraries online.[3]

For the more exotic characters there is often not much choice. We have had success using Michael Everson's Everson Mono font, which has 9,756 different glyphs (not including Chinese)[4] and with the somewhat older Titus Cyberbit

[2] https://www.google.com/get/noto/

[3] http://unicode.org/resources/fonts.html

[4] http://www.evertype.com/emono/

Basic font by Jost Gippert and Carl-Martin Bunz. It includes 10,044 different glyphs (not including Chinese).[5]

We also suggest installing at least one fall-back font, which provides glyphs that show the user some information about the underlying encoded character. Apple computers have such a font (which is invisible to the user), which is designed by Michael Everson and made available for other systems through the Unicode Consortium.[6] Further, the GNU Unifont is a clever way to produce bitmaps approximating the intended glyph of each available character.[7] Finally, SIL International provides a SIL Unicode BMP Fallback Font. This font does not show a real glyph, but instead shows the hexadecimal code inside a box for each character, so a user can at least see the Unicode code point of the character intended for display.[8]

3.5 Pitfall: Faulty rendering

A similar complaint to missing glyphs, discussed previously, is that while a glyph might be displayed, it does not look right. There are two reasons for unexpected visual display, namely automatic font substitution and faulty rendering. Like missing glyphs, any such problems are independent from the Unicode Standard. The Unicode Standard only includes very general information about characters and leaves the specific visual display for others to decide on. Any faulty display is thus not to be blamed on the Unicode Consortium, but on a complex interplay of different mechanisms happening in a computer to turn Unicode code points into visual symbols. We will only sketch a few aspects of this complex interplay here.

Most modern software applications (like Microsoft Word) offer some approach to automatic font substitution. This means that when a text is written in a specific font (e.g. Times New Roman) and an inserted Unicode character does not have a glyph within this font, then the software application will automatically search for another font to display the glyph. The result will be that this specific glyph will look slightly different from the others. This mechanism works differently depending on the software application; only limited user influence is usually expected and little feedback is given. This may be rather frustrating to font-aware users.

[5]http://titus.fkidg1.uni-frankfurt.de/unicode/tituut.asp

[6]http://www.unicode.org/policies/lastresortfont_eula.html

[7]http://unifoundry.com/unifont.html

[8]http://scripts.sil.org/UnicodeBMPFallbackFont

Another problem with visual display is related to so-called FONT RENDERING. Font rendering refers to the process of the actual positioning of Unicode characters on a page of written text. This positioning is actually a highly complex challenge and many things can go wrong in the process. Well-known rendering difficulties, like proportional glyph size or ligatures, are reasonably well understood by developers. Nevertheless, the positioning of multiple diacritics relative to a base character is still a widespread problem. Especially problematic is when more than one diacritic is supposed to be placed above (or below) another. Even within the Latin script vertical placement often leads to unexpected effects in many modern software applications. The rendering problems arising in Arabic and in many scripts of Southeast Asia (like Devanagari or Burmese) are even more complex.

To understand why these problems arise it is important to realize that there are basically three different approaches to font rendering. The most widespread is Adobe's and Microsoft's OPENTYPE system. This approach makes it relatively easy for font developers, but the font itself does not include all details about the precise placement of individual characters. For those details, additional script descriptions are necessary. All such systems can lead to unexpected behavior.[9] Alternative systems are APPLE ADVANCED TYPOGRAPHY (AAT) and the open-source GRAPHITE system produced and maintained by the Non-Roman Script Initiative of SIL International (SIL).[10] In these systems, a larger burden is placed on the description inside the font.

There is no complete solution to the problems arising from faulty font rendering. Switching to another software application that offers better handling is the only real alternative, but this is normally not an option for daily work. Font rendering is developing quickly in the software industry, so we can expect the situation to only get better.

3.6 Pitfall: Blocks

The Unicode code space is subdivided into blocks of contiguous code points. For example, the block called CYRILLIC runs from U+0400 till U+04FF. These blocks

[9] For more details about OpenType, see http://www.adobe.com/products/type/opentype.html and http://www.microsoft.com/typography/otspec/. Additional systems for complex text layout are, among others, Microsoft's DirectWrite (https://msdn.microsoft.com/library/dd368038.aspx) and the open-source project HarfBuzz (http://www.freedesktop.org/wiki/Software/HarfBuzz/).

[10] More information about AAT can be found at: https://developer.apple.com/fonts/.
Graphite is described in detail at: http://scripts.sil.org/default.

arose as an attempt at ordering the enormous number of characters in Unicode, but the idea of blocks very quickly ran into problems. First, the size of a block is fixed, so when a block is full, a new block will have to be instantiated somewhere else in the code space. For example, this led to the blocks Cyrillic Supplement, Cyrillic Extended-A (both of which are already full) and Cyrillic Extended-B. Second, when a specific character already exists, it is not duplicated in another block, although the name of the block might indicate that a specific symbol should be available there. In general, names of blocks are just an approximate indication of the kind of characters that will be in the block.

The problem with blocks arises because finding the right character among the thousands of Unicode characters is not easy. Many software applications present blocks as a primary search mechanism, because the block names suggest where to look for a particular character. However, when a user searches for an IPA character in the block IPA Extensions, then many IPA characters will not be found there. For example, the velar nasal <ŋ> is not part of the block IPA Extensions because it was already included as LATIN SMALL LETTER ENG at U+014B in the block Latin Extensions-A.

In general, finding a specific character in the Unicode Standard is often non-trivial. The names of the blocks can help, but they are not (and were never supposed to be) a foolproof structure. It is neither the goal nor the aim of the Unicode Consortium to provide a user interface to the Unicode Standard. If one often encounters the problem of needing to find a suitable character, there are various other useful services for end-users available.[11]

3.7 Pitfall: Names

The names of characters in the Unicode Standard are sometimes misnomers and should not be misinterpreted as definitions. For example, the COMBINING GRAPHEME JOINER at U+034F does not join characters into larger graphemes (see Section 3.3) and the LATIN LETTER RETROFLEX CLICK U+01C3 is actually not the IPA symbol for a retroflex click, but for an alveolar click (see Section 5.3). In a sense, these names can be seen as errors. However, it is probably better to realize that

[11]The Unicode website offers a basic interface to the code charts at: http://www.unicode.org/charts/index.html. As a more flexible interface, we particularly like PopChar from Ergonis Software, available for both Mac and Windows. There are also various free websites that offer search interfaces to the Unicode code tables, like http://unicode-search.net or http://unicode-search.net. Another useful approach for searching for characters using shape matching (Belongie et al. 2002) is: http://shapecatcher.com.

such names are just convenience labels that are not going to be changed. Just like the block names (Section 3.6), the character names are often helpful, but they are not supposed to be definitions.

The actual intended meaning of a Unicode code point is a combination of the name, the block and the character properties (see Chapter 2). Further details about the underlying intentions with which a character should be used are only accessible by perusing the actual decisions of the Unicode Consortium. All proposals, discussions and decisions of the Unicode Consortium are publicly available. Unfortunately there is not (yet) any way to easily find everything that is ever proposed, discussed and decided in relation to a specific code point of interest, so many of the details are often somewhat hidden.[12]

3.8 Pitfall: Homoglyphs

Homoglyphs are visually indistinguishable glyphs (or highly similar glyphs) that have different code points in the Unicode Standard and thus different character semantics. As a principle, the Unicode Standard does not specify how a character appears visually on the page or the screen. So in most cases, a different appearance is caused by the specific design of a font, or by user-settings like size or boldface. Taking an example already discussed in Section 2.3, the following symbols <g g g g g g> are different glyphs of the same character, i.e. they may be rendered differently depending on the typography being used, but they all share the same code point (viz. LATIN SMALL LETTER G at U+0067). In contrast, the symbols <AAAAAᴀAAAA> are all different code points, although they look highly similar – in some cases even sharing exactly the same glyph in some fonts. All these different A-like characters include the following code points in the Unicode Standard:

<A> LATIN CAPITAL LETTER A, at U+0041
<А> CYRILLIC CAPITAL LETTER A, at U+0410
<Α> GREEK CAPITAL LETTER ALPHA, at U+0391
<Ꭺ> CHEROKEE LETTER GO, at U+13AA
<ᗅ> CANADIAN SYLLABICS CARRIER GHO, at U+15C5
<ᴀ> LATIN SMALL LETTER CAPITAL A, at U+1D00

[12] All proposals and other documents that are the basis of Unicode decisions are available at: http://www.unicode.org/L2/all-docs.html. The actual decisions that make up the Unicode Standard are documented in the minutes of the Unicode Technical Committee, available at: http://www.unicode.org/consortium/utc-minutes.html.

<A> LISU LETTER A, at U+A4EE
<A> CARIAN LETTER A, at U+102A0
<A> MATHEMATICAL SANS-SERIF CAPITAL A, U+1D5A0
<A> MATHEMATICAL MONOSPACE CAPITAL A, at U+1D670

The existence of such homoglyphs is partly due to legacy compatibility, but for the most part these characters are simply different characters that happen to look similar.[13] Yet, they are suppose to behave differently from the perspective of a font designer. For example, when designing a Cyrillic font, the <A> will have different aesthetics and different traditional expectations compared to a Latin <A>. Thus, the Unicode Standard has character properties associated with each code point which define certain expectations, e.g. characters belong to different blocks, they have different lower case variants (see Section 2.3).

Homoglyphs are a widespread problem for consistent encoding. Although for most users it looks like the words <voces> and <voces> are nearly identical, in fact they do not share any code points.[14] For computers these two words are completely different entities. Sometimes when users with Cyrillic or Greek keyboards have to type some Latin-based orthography, they mix similar looking Cyrillic or Greek characters into their text, because those characters are so much easier to type. Similarly, when users want to enter an unusual symbol, they normally search by visual impression in their favorite software application, and just pick something that looks reasonably alike to what they expect the glyph to look like.

It is very easy to make errors during text entry and add characters that are not supposed to be included. Our proposals for orthography profiles (see Chapter 7) are a method for checking the consistency of any text. In situations in which interoperability is important, we consider it crucial to add such checks in any workflow.

3.9 Pitfall: Canonical equivalence

For some characters, there is more than one possible encoding in the Unicode Standard. This means that for the computer there exists multiple different entities, which for the user, may be visually the same. This leads to, for example,

[13] A particularly nice interface to look for homoglyphs is http://shapecatcher.com, based on the principle of recognizing shapes (Belongie et al. 2002).

[14] The first words consists completely of Latin characters: U+0076, U+006F, U+0063, U+0065 and U+0073. The second is a mix of Cyrillic and Greek characters: U+03BD, U+03BF, U+0041, U+0435 and U+0455.

problems with search. The computer searches for specific code points and by design does not return all visually similar characters. As a solution, the Unicode Standard includes a notion of CANONICAL EQUIVALENCE. Different encodings are explicitly declared as equivalent in the Unicode Standard code tables. Further, to harmonize all encodings in a specific piece of text, the Unicode Standard proposes a mechanism of NORMALIZATION. The process of normalization and the Unicode Normalization Forms are described in detail in the Unicode Standard Annex #15 online.[15] Here we provide a brief summary of that material as it pertains to canonical equivalence.

Consider for example the characters and following Unicode code points:

1. <Å> LATIN CAPITAL LETTER A WITH RING ABOVE U+00C5
2. <Å> ANGSTROM SIGN U+212B
3. <Å> LATIN CAPITAL LETTER A U+0041 + COMBINING RING ABOVE U+030A

The character, represented here by glyph <Å>, is encoded in the Unicode Standard in the first two examples by a single-character sequence; each is assigned a different code point. In the third example, the glyph is encoded in a multiple-character sequence that is composed of two character code points. All three sequences are , i.e. they are strings that represent the same abstract character and because they are not distinguishable by the user, the Unicode Standard requires them to be treated the same in regards to their behavior and appearance. Nevertheless, they are encoded differently. For example, if one were to search an electronic text (with software that does not apply Unicode Standard normalization) for ANGSTROM SIGN (U+212B), then the instances of LATIN CAPITAL LETTER A WITH RING ABOVE (U+00C5) would not be found.

In other words, there are equivalent sequences of Unicode characters that should be normalized, i.e. transformed into a unique Unicode-sanctioned representation of a character sequence called a NORMALIZATION FORM. Unicode provides a Unicode Normalization Algorithm, which puts combining marks into a specific logical order and it defines decomposition and composition transformation rules to convert each string into one of four normalization forms. We will discuss here the two most relevant normalization forms: NFC and NFD.

The first of the three characters above is considered the NORMALIZATION FORM C (NFC), where C stands for composition. When the process of NFC normalization is applied to the characters in 2 and 3, both are normalized into the PRECOMPOSED character sequence in 1. Thus all three canonical character sequences

[15] http://unicode.org/reports/tr15/

are standardized into one composition form in NFC. The other frequently encountered Unicode normalization form is the Normalization Form D (NFD), where D stands for decomposition. When NFD is applied to the three examples above, all three, including importantly the single-character sequences in 1 and 2, are normalized into the decomposed multiple-sequence of characters in 3. Again, all three are then logically equivalent and therefore comparable and syntactically interoperable.

As illustrated, some characters in the Unicode Standard have alternative representations (in fact, many do), but the Unicode Normalization Algorithm can be used to transform certain sequences of characters into canonical forms to test for equivalency. To determine equivalence, each character in the Unicode Standard is associated with a combining class, which is formally defined as a character property called canonical combining class which is specified in the Unicode Character Database. The combining class assigned to each code point is a numeric value between 0 and 254 and is used by the Unicode Canonical Ordering Algorithm to determine which sequences of characters are . Normalization forms, as very briefly described above, can be used to ensure character equivalence by ordering character sequences so that they can be faithfully compared.

It is very important to note that any software application that is Unicode Standard compliant is free to change the character stream from one representation to another. This means that a software application may compose, decompose or reorder characters as its developers desire; as long as the resultant strings are to the original. This might lead to unexpected behavior for users. Various players, like the Unicode Consortium, the W3C, or the TEI recommend NFC in most user-directed situations, and some software applications that we tested indeed seem to automatically convert strings into NFC.[16] This means in practice that if a user, for example, enters <a> and <◌̀>, i.e. latin small letter a at U+0061 and combining grave accent at U+0300, this might be automatically converted into <à>, i.e. latin small letter a with grave at U+00E0.[17]

[16] See the summary of various recommendation here: http://www.win.tue.nl/~aeb/linux/uc/nfc_vs_nfd.html.

[17] The behavior of software applications can be quite erratic in this respect. For example, Apple's TextEdit does not do any conversion on text entry. However, when you copy and paste some text inside the same document in rich text mode (i.e. RTF-format), it will be transformed into NFC on paste. Saving a document does not do any conversion to the glyphs on screen, but it will save the characters in NFC.

3.10 Pitfall: Absence of canonical equivalence

Although in most cases canonical equivalence will take care of alternative encodings of the same character, there are some cases in which the Unicode Standard decided against equivalence. This leads to identical characters that are not equivalent, like <ø> LATIN SMALL LETTER O WITH STROKE at U+00F8 and <o̷> a combination of LATIN SMALL LETTER O at U+006F with COMBINING SHORT SOLIDUS OVERLAY at U+0037. The general rule followed is that extensions of Latin characters that are connected to the base character are not separated as combining diacritics. For example, characters like <ŋ ɲ ɳ> or <ɖ ɗ> are obviously derived from <n> and <d> respectively, but they are treated like new separate characters in the Unicode Standard. Likewise, characters like <ø> and <ƈ> are not separated into a base character <o> and <c> with an attached combining diacritic.

Interestingly, and somewhat illogically, there are three elements which are directly attached to their base characters, but which are still treated as separable in the Unicode Standard. Such characters are decomposed (in NFD normalization) into a base character with a combining diacritic. However, it is these cases that should be considered the exceptions to the rule. These three elements are the following:

- <◌̧>: the COMBINING CEDILLA at U+0327
  This diacritic is for example attested in the precomposed character <ç> LATIN SMALL LETTER C WITH CEDILLA at U+00E7. This <ç> will thus be decomposed in NFC normalization.
- <◌̨>: the COMBINING OGONEK at U+0328
  This diacritic is for example attested in precomposed <ą> LATIN SMALL LETTER A WITH OGONEK at U+0105. This <ą> will thus be decomposed in NFC normalization.
- <◌̛>: the COMBINING HORN at U+031B
  This diacritic is for example attested in precomposed <ơ> LATIN SMALL LETTER O WITH HORN at U+01A1. This <ơ> will thus be decomposed in NFC normalization.

There are further combinations that deserve special care because it is actually possible to produce identical characters in different ways without them being . In these situations, the general rule holds, namely that characters with attached extras are not decomposed. However, in the following cases the extras actually exist as combining diacritics, so there is also the possibility to construct a character by using a base character with those combining diacritics.

- First, there are the combining characters designated as *combining overlay* in the Unicode Standard, like <◌̴> COMBINING TILDE OVERLAY at U+0334 or <◌̵> COMBINING SHORT STROKE OVERLAY at U+0335. There are many characters that look like they are precomposed with such an overlay, for example <ɫ ƀ đ ꝑ> or <ƚ ɨ ɉ ɍ>, or also the example of <ø> given at the start of this section. However, they are not decomposed in NFD normalization.
- Second, the same situation also occurs with combining characters designated as *combining hook*, like <◌̡> COMBINING PALATALIZED HOOK BELOW at U+0321. This element seems to occur in precomposed characters like <ᶀ ᶁ ᶂ ᶄ>. However, they are not decomposed in NFD normalization.

To harmonize the encoding in these cases it is not sufficient to use Unicode normalization. Additional checks are necessary, for example by using orthography profiles (see Chapter 7).

3.11 Pitfall: Encodings

Before we discuss the pitfall of different file formats in Section 3.12, it is pertinent to point out that the common usage of the term ENCODING unfortunately does not distinguish between *encoded* sequences of code points and text *encoded* as bit patterns. Recall, a code point is simply a numerical representation of some defined entity; in other words, a code point is a character encoding-specific unique identifier or ID. In the Unicode Standard encoding, code points are numbers that serve as unique identifiers, each of which is associated with a set of character properties defined by the Unicode Consortium in the Unicode Character Database.[18] The number of each code point can be *encoded* in various formats, including as a decimal integer (e.g. 112), as an 8-bit binary sequence (01110000) or hexadecimal (0070). This example Unicode code point, U+0070, represents LATIN SMALL LETTER P and its associated Unicode properties, such as it belongs to the category Letter, Lowercase [Ll], in the Basic Latin block, and that its title case and upper case is associated with code point U+0050.[19]

The other meaning of encoding has to do with the fact that computers represent data and instructions in patterns of bits. A bit pattern is a combination of binary digits arranged in a sequence. And how these sequences are carved up into bit patterns is determined by how they are *encoded*. Thus the term ENCODING is used for both sequences of code points and text encoded as bit patterns. Hence

---

[18] https://www.unicode.org/ucd/

[19] See also Chapter 2.

a Unicode-aware programmer might prefer to say that UTF-8, UTF-16, etc., are Unicode encoding systems because they determine how sequences of bit patterns are determined, which are then mapped to characters.[20] The terminological issue here is that the Unicode Standard introduces a layer of indirection between characters and bit patterns, i.e. the code point, which can be encoded differently by different encoding systems.

Note also that all computer character encodings include so-called CONTROL CHARACTERS, which are non-printable sometimes action-inducing characters, such as the null character, bell code, backspace, escape, delete, and line feed. Control characters can interact with encoding schemes. For example, some programming languages make use of the null character to mark the end of a string. Line breaks are part of the text, and as such as covered by the Unicode Standard. But they can be problematic because line breaks differ from operating system to operating system in how they are encoded. These variants are discussed in Section 3.12.

3.12 Pitfall: File formats

Unicode is a character encoding standard, but characters of course appear inside some kind of computer file. The most basic Unicode-based file format is pure line-based text, i.e. strings of Unicode-encoded characters separated by line breaks (note that these line breaks are what for most people intuitively corresponds to paragraph breaks). Unfortunately, even within this apparently basic setting there exists a multitude of variants. In general these different possibilities are well-understood in the software industry, and nowadays they normally do not lead to any problems for the end user. However, there are some situations in which a user is suddenly confronted with cryptic questions in the user interface involving abbreviations like LF, CR, BE, LE or BOM. Most prominently this occurs with exporting or importing data in several software applications from Microsoft. Basically, there are two different issues involved. First, the encoding of line breaks and, second, the encoding of the Unicode characters into code units and the related issue of endianness.

[20]UTF stands for Unicode Transformation Format. It a method for translating numbers into binary data and vice versa. There are several different UTF encoding formats, e.g. UTF-8 is a variable-length encoding that uses 8-bit code units, is compatible with ASCII, and is common on the web. UTF-16 is also variable-length, uses 16-bit code units, and is used system-internally by Windows and Java. See further discussion under *Code units* in Section 3.12. For more in-depth discussion, refer to the Unicode Frequently Asked Questions and additional sources therein: http://unicode.org/faq/utf_bom.html.

Line breaks

The issue with LINE BREAKS originated with the instructions necessary to direct a printing head of a physical printer to a new line. This involves two movements, known as CARRIAGE RETURN (CR, returning the printing head to the start of the line on the page) and LINE FEED (LF, moving the printing head to the next line on the page). Physically, these are two different events, but conceptually together they form one action. In the history of computing, various encodings of line breaks have been used (e.g. CR+LF, LF+CR, only LF, or only CR). Currently, all Unix and Unix-derived systems use only LF as code for a line break, while software from Microsoft still uses a combination of CR+LF. Today, most software applications recognize both options, and are able to deal with either encoding of line breaks (until rather recently this was not the case, and using the wrong line breaks would lead to unexpected errors). Our impression is that there is a strong tendency in software development to standardize on the simpler "only LF" encoding for line breaks, and we suggest that everybody should use this encoding whenever possible.

Code units

The issue with CODE UNITS stems from the question how to separate a stream of binary ones and zeros, i.e. bits, into chunks representing Unicode characters. A code unit is the sequence of bits used to encode a single character in an encoding. The Unicode Standard offers three different approaches, called UTF-32, UTF-16 and UTF-8, that are intended for different use cases.[21] The details of this issue are extensively explained in section 2.5 of the Unicode Core Specification (The Unicode Consortium 2018).

Basically, UTF-32 encodes each character in 32 bits (32 *bi*nary uni*ts*, i.e. 32 zeros or ones) and is the most disk-space-consuming variant of the three. However, it is the most efficient encoding processing-wise, because the computer simply has to separate each character after 32 bits.

In contrast, UTF-16 uses only 16 bits per character, which is sufficient for the large majority of Unicode characters, but not for all of them. A special system of SURROGATES is defined within the Unicode Standard to deal with these additional characters. The effect is a more disk-space efficient encoding (approximately half

[21]The letters UTF stand for UNICODE TRANSFORMATION FORMAT, but the notion of "transformation" is a legacy notion that does not have meaning anymore. Nevertheless, the designation UTF (in capitals) has become an official standard designation, but should probably best be read as simply "Unicode Format".

the size), while adding a limited computational overhead to manage the surrogates.

Finally, UTF-8 is a more complex system that dynamically encodes each character with the minimally necessary number of bits, choosing either 8, 16 or 32 bits depending on the character. This represents again a strong reduction in space (particularly due to the high frequency of data using erstwhile ASCII characters, which need only 8 bits) at the expense of even more computation necessary to process such strings. However, because of the ever growing computational power of modern machines, the processing overhead is in most practical situations a non-issue, while saving on space is still useful, particularly for sending texts over the Internet. As a result, UTF-8 has become the dominant encoding on the World Wide Web. We suggest that everybody uses UTF-8 as their default encoding.

A related problem is a general issue about how to store information in computer memory, which is known as ENDIANNESS. The details of this issue go beyond the scope of this book. It suffices to realize that there is a difference between BIG-ENDIAN (BE) storage and LITTLE-ENDIAN (LE) storage. The Unicode Standard offers a possibility to explicitly indicate what kind of storage is used by starting a file with a so-called BYTE ORDER MARK (BOM). However, the Unicode Standard does not require the use of BOM, preferring other non-Unicode methods to signal to computers which kind of endianness is used. This issue only arises with UTF-32 and UTF-16 encodings. When using the preferred UTF-8, using a BOM is theoretically possible, but strongly dispreferred according to the Unicode Standard. We suggest that everyone tries to prevent the inclusion of BOM in their data.

3.13 Pitfall: Incomplete implementations

Another pitfall that we encounter when using the Unicode Standard is its incomplete implementation in different standards and programming languages, e.g. SQL, XML, XLST, Python. For example, although the Unicode Standard mandates that the comparison of Unicode text be done using normalized text, this is not the case with the equality operator "==" in Python. Furthermore, it is not always transparent what the operating system or specific software applications do when text is being copied and pasted. For example, copy and pasting the character sequence U+0061 LATIN SMALL LETTER A <a> and U+0301 COMBINING ACUTE ACCENT <◌́>, visually <á>, into the text editor TextWrangler leaves the sequence decomposed as two characters. But when pasting the decomposed sequence into

RStudio, and other software programs, the sequence becomes precomposed as U+00E1 LATIN SMALL LETTER A WITH ACUTE, i.e. <á>.

3.14 Recommendations

Summarizing the pitfalls discussed in this chapter, we propose the following recommendations:

- To prevent strange boxes instead of nice glyphs, always install a few fonts with a large glyph collection and at least one fall-back font (see Section 3.4).
- Unexpected visual impressions of symbols do not necessarily mean that the actual encoding is wrong. It is mostly a problem of faulty rendering (see Section 3.5).
- Do not trust the names of code points as a definition of the character (see Section 3.7). Also do not trust Unicode blocks as a strategy to find specific characters (see Section 3.6).
- To ensure consistent encoding of texts, apply Unicode normalization (NFC or NFD, see Section 3.9).
- To prevent remaining inconsistencies after normalization, for example stemming from homoglyphs (see Section 3.8) or from missing canonical equivalence in the Unicode Standard (see Section 3.10), use orthography profiles (see Chapter 7).
- To deal with tailored grapheme clusters (Section 3.3), use Unicode Locale Descriptions, or orthography profiles (see Chapter 7).
- As a preferred file format, use Unicode Format UTF-8 in Normalization Form Composition (NFC) with LF line endings, but without byte order mark (BOM), whenever possible (see Section 3.12). This last nicely cryptic recommendation has T-shirt potential:

I prefer it
UTF-8 NFC LF no BOM

4 The International Phonetic Alphabet

In this chapter we present a brief history of the IPA (Section 4.1), which dates back to the late 19th century, not long after the creation of the first typewriter with a QWERTY keyboard. An understanding of the IPA and its premises and principles (Section 4.2) leads to a better appreciation of the challenges that the International Phonetic Association faced when digitally encoding the IPA's set of symbols and diacritics (Section 4.3). Occurring a little over a hundred years after the inception of the IPA, its encoding was a major challenge (Section 4.4); many linguists have encountered the pitfalls when the two are used together (Chapter 5).

4.1 Brief history

Established in 1886, the INTERNATIONAL PHONETIC ASSOCIATION (henceforth *Association*) has long maintained a standard alphabet, the INTERNATIONAL PHONETIC ALPHABET or IPA, which is a standard in linguistics to transcribe sounds of spoken languages. It was first published in 1888 as an international system of phonetic transcription for oral languages and for pedagogical purposes. It contained phonetic values for English, French and German. Diacritics for length and nasalization were already present in this first version, and the same symbols are still used today.

Originally, the IPA was a list of symbols with pronunciation examples using words in different languages. In 1900 the symbols were first organized into a chart and were given phonetic feature labels, e.g. for manner of articulation among others *plosives, nasales, fricatives*, for place of articulation among others *bronchiales, laryngales, labiales* and for vowels e.g. *fermées, mi-fermées, mi-ouvertes, ouvertes.* Throughout the last century, the structure of the chart has changed with increases in phonetic knowledge. Thus, similar to notational systems in other scientific disciplines, the IPA reflects facts and theories of phonetic knowledge that have developed over time. It is natural then that the IPA is modified occasionally to accommodate scientific innovations and discoveries. In fact, updates are part of the Association's mandate. These changes are captured in revisions to the IPA chart.[1]

Over the years there have been several revisions, but mostly minor ones. Articulation labels – what are often called *features* even though the IPA deliberately avoids this term – have changed, e.g. terms like *lips*, *throat* or *rolled* are no longer used. Phonetic symbol values have changed, e.g. voiceless is no longer marked by <h>. Symbols have been dropped, e.g. the caret diacritic denoting 'long and narrow' is no longer used. And many symbols have been added to reflect contrastive sounds found in the world's very diverse phonological systems. The use of the IPA is guided by principles outlined in the *Handbook of the International Phonetic Association* (The International Phonetic Association 1999), henceforth simply called *Handbook*.

Today, the IPA is designed to meet practical linguistic needs and is used to transcribe the phonetic or phonological structure of languages. It is also used increasingly as a foreign language learning tool, as a standard pronunciation guide and as a tool for creating practical orthographies of previously unwritten languages. The IPA suits many linguists' needs because:

- it is intended to be a set of symbols for representing all possible sounds in the world's (spoken) languages;
- its chart has a linguistic basis (and specifically a phonological bias) rather than just being a general phonetic notation scheme;
- its symbols can be used to represent distinctive feature combinations;[2]
- its chart provides a summary of linguists' agreed-upon phonetic knowledge.

Several styles of transcription with the IPA are possible, as illustrated in the *Handbook*, and they are all valid.[3] Therefore, there are different but equivalent transcriptions, or as noted by Ladefoged (1990: 64), "perhaps now that the Association has been explicit in its eclectic approach, outsiders to the Association will no longer speak of *the* IPA transcription of a given phenomenon, as if there were only one approved style." Clearly not all phoneticians agree, nor are they likely

[1]For a detailed history, we refer the reader to: https://en.wikipedia.org/wiki/History_of_the_International_Phonetic_Alphabet.

[2]Although the chart uses traditional manner and place of articulation labels, the symbols can be used as a representation of any defined bundle of features, binary or otherwise, to define phonetic dimensions.

[3]For an illustration of the differences, see the 29 languages and their transcriptions in the *Illustrations of the IPA* (The International Phonetic Association 1999: 41–154).

to ever completely agree, on all aspects of the IPA or on transcription approaches and practices in general. As noted above, there have been several revisions in the IPA's long history, but the current version (2005) is strikingly similar to the 1926 version, which shows the viability of the IPA as a common standard for linguistic transcription.

4.2 Premises and principles

Premises

Any IPA transcription is based on two premises: (i) that it is possible to describe the acoustic speech signal (sound waves) in terms of sequentially ordered discrete segments, and, (ii) that each segment can be characterized by an articulatory target.

Once spoken language data are segmented, the IPA provides symbols to unambiguously represent phonetic details. However, since phonetic detail could potentially include anything, e.g. something like "deep voice", the IPA restricts phonetic detail to linguistically relevant aspects of speech. Phonological considerations thus inextricably play a roll in transcription. In other words, phonetic observations beyond quantitative acoustic analysis are always made in terms of some phonological framework.

Today, the IPA chart reflects a linguistic theory grounded in principles of phonological contrast and in knowledge about the attested linguistic variation. This fact is stated explicitly in several places, including in the *Report on the 1989 Kiel convention* published in the *Journal of the International Phonetic Association* (Roach 1989: 67–68):

> The IPA is intended to be a set of symbols for representing all the possible sounds of the world's languages. The representation of these sounds uses a set of phonetic categories which describe how each sound is made. These categories define a number of natural classes of sounds that operate in phonological rules and historical sound changes. The symbols of the IPA are shorthand ways of indicating certain intersections of these categories.

and in the *Handbook* (The International Phonetic Association 1999: 18):

> [...] a symbol can be regarded as a shorthand equivalent to a phonetic description, and a way of representing the contrasting sounds that occur in a language. Thus [m] is equivalent to "voiced bilabial nasal", and is also a

> way of representing one of the contrasting nasal sounds that occur in English and other languages. [...] When a symbol is said to be suitable for the representation of sounds in two languages, it does not necessarily mean that the sounds in the two languages are identical.

From its earliest days the Association aimed to provide "a separate sign for each distinctive sound; that is, for each sound which, being used instead of another, in the same language, can change the meaning of a word" (The International Phonetic Association 1999: 27). Distinctive sounds became later known as PHONEMES and the IPA has developed historically into a notational device with a strictly segmental phonemic view. A phoneme is an abstract theoretical notion derived from an acoustic signal as produced by speakers in the real world. Therefore the IPA contains a number of theoretical assumptions about speech and how to transcribe speech in written form.

Principles

Essentially, transcription has two parts: a text containing symbols and a set of conventions for interpreting those symbols (and their combinations). The symbols of the IPA distinguish between letter-like symbols and diacritics (symbol modifiers). The use of the letter-like symbols to represent a language's sounds is guided by the principle of contrast; where two words are distinguishable by phonemic contrast, those contrasts should be transcribed with different letter symbols (and not just diacritics). Allophonic distinction falls under the rubric of diacritically-distinguished symbols, e.g. the difference in English between an aspirated /p/ in [pʰæt] and an unreleased /p/ in [stop̚].

- Different letter-like symbols should be used whenever a language employs two sounds contrastively.
- When two sounds in a language are not known to be contrastive, the same symbol should be used to represent these sounds. Diacritics may be used to distinguish different articulations when necessary.

Yet, in some situations diacritics are used to mark phonemic contrasts. The *Handbook* recommends to limit the use of phonemic diacritics to the following situations:

- denoting length, stress and pitch;
- obviating the design of a (large) number of new symbols when a single diacritic suffices (e.g. nasalized vowels, aspirated stops).

The interpretation of the IPA symbols in specific usage is not trivial. Although the articulatory properties of the IPA symbols themselves are rather succinctly summarized by the normative description in the *Handbook*, it is common in practical applications that the transcribed symbols do not precisely represent the phonetic value of the sounds that they represent. So an IPA symbol <t> in one transcription is not always the same as an IPA <t> in another transcription (or even within a single transcription). The interpretation of any particular <t> is mostly a language-specific convention (or even resource-specific and possibly even context-specific), a fact which – unfortunately – is in most cases not made explicit by users of the IPA.

There are different reasons for this difficulty to interpret IPA symbols, all officially sanctioned by the IPA. An important principle of the IPA is that different representations resulting from different underlying analyses are allowed. Because the IPA does not provide phonological analyses for specific languages, the IPA does not define a single correct transcription system. Rather, the IPA aims to provide a resource that allows users to express any analysis so that it is widely understood. Basically, the IPA allows for both a *narrow* phonetic transcription and a *broad* phonological transcription. A narrow phonetic transcription may freely use all symbols in the IPA chart with direct reference to their phonetic value, i.e. the transcriber can indicate with the symbols <ŋ͡m> that the phonetic value of the attested sound is a simultaneous labial and velar closure which is voiced and contains nasal airflow, independently of the phonemic status of this sound in the language in question.

In contrast, the basic goal of a broad phonemic transcription is to distinguish all words in a language with a minimal number of transcription symbols (Abercrombie 1964: 19). A phonemic transcription includes the conventions of a particular language's phonological rules. These rules determine the realization of that language's phonemes. For example, in the transcription of German, Dutch, English and French a symbol <t> might be used for the voiceless plosive in the alveolar and dental areas. This symbol is sufficient for a succinct transcription of these languages because there is no further phonemic subdivisions in this domain in either of these languages. However, the language-specific realization of this consonant is closer to [t̪ʰ], [t], [tʰ] and [t̪], respectively. Similarly, the five vowels of Greek can be represented phonemically in IPA as /ieaou/, though phonetically they are closer to [iɛaɔu]. The Japanese five-vowel system can also be transcribed in IPA as /ieaou/, while the phonetic targets in this case are closer to [ieaoɯ].

Note also that there can be different systems of phonemic transcription for the same variety of a language, so two different resources on the "same" language might use different symbols that represent the same sound. The differences may result from the fact that more than one phonetic symbol may be appropriate for a phoneme, or the differences may be due to different phonemic analyses, e.g. Standard German's vowel system is arguably contrastive in length, tenseness or vowel quality. Finally, even within a single phonemic transcription a specific symbol can have different realizations because of allophonic variation which might not be explicitly transcribed.

In sum, there are three different reasons why phonemically-based IPA transcription is difficult to interpret:

- A symbol represents the phonemic status, and not necessarily the precise phonetic realization. So, different transcriptions might use the same symbol for different underlying sounds.
- Any symbol that is used for a specific phoneme is not necessarily unique, so different transcriptions might use different symbols for the same underlying sound.
- Allophonic variation can be disregarded in phonemic transcription, so the same symbol within a single transcription can represent different sounds.

Ideally, all such implicit conventions of a phonemic transcription would be explicitly codified. This could very well be performed by using an orthography profile (see Chapter 7), linking the selected phonemic transcription symbols to narrow phonetic transcriptions, possibly also including specifications of contextual interpretation.

4.3 IPA encodings

In 1989, an IPA revision convention was held in Kiel, Germany. As in previous meetings, there were changes made to the repertoire of phonetic symbols in the IPA chart, which reflected what had been discovered, described and cataloged by linguists about the phonological systems in the world's languages in the interim. Personal computers were also becoming more commonplace, and linguists were using them to create databases. A cogent example is the UCLA Phonological Segment Inventory Database (UPSID; Maddieson 1984), which was expanded (Maddieson & Precoda 1990) and then encoded and distributed in a computer program (Maddieson & Precoda 1992).[4] The programmers used only ASCII characters to maximize compatibility (e.g. <kpW> for [kpʷ]), but were faced with unavoidable arbitrary mappings between ASCII letters and punctuation, and the more than 900 segment types documented in their sample of world's languages' phonological systems. The developers devised a system of base characters with secondary diacritic marks (e.g. in the previous example <kp>, the base character, is modified with <W>). This encoding approach is also used in SAMPA and X-SAMPA (Section 4.3) and in the ASJP.[5] But before UPSID, SAMPA and ASJP, IPA was encoded with numbers.

IPA Numbers

Prior to the Kiel Convention for the modern revision of the IPA in 1989, Wells (1987) collected and published practical approaches to coded representations of the IPA, which dealt mainly with the assignment of characters on the keyboard to IPA symbols. The process of assigning standardized computer codes to phonetic symbols was given to the *workgroup on computer coding* (henceforth *working group*) at the Kiel Convention. This working group was given the following tasks (Esling 1990; Esling & Gaylord 1993):

- determining how to represent the IPA numerically
- developing a set of numbers to refer to the IPA symbols unambiguously
- providing each symbol a unique name (intended to provide a mnemonic description of that character's shape)

The identification of IPA symbols with unique identifiers was a first step in formalizing the IPA computationally because it would give each symbol an unambiguous numerical identifier called an IPA NUMBER. The numbering system was to be comprehensive enough to support future revisions of the IPA, including symbol specifications and diacritic placement. The application of diacritics was also to be made explicit.

Although the Association had never officially approved a set of names for the IPA symbols, each IPA symbol received a unique IPA NAME. Many symbols already had an informal name (or two) used by linguists, but consensus on symbol names was growing due to the recent publication of the *Phonetic Symbol Guide*

[4]It could be installed via floppy disk on an IBM PC, or compatible, running DOS with 1MB free disk space and 360K available RAM.

[5]See the ASJP use case in the online supplementary materials to this book: https://github.com/unicode-cookbook/recipes.

(Pullum & Ladusaw 1986). Thus most of the IPA symbol names were taken from that source (The International Phonetic Association 1999: 31).

The working group decided insightfully that the computing-coding convention for the IPA should be independent of computer environments or formats, i.e. the IPA NUMBER was not meant to be encoded at the bit pattern level. The working group report's declaration includes the following explanatory remarks (Roach 1989: 82):

> The recommendation of a 7-bit ASCII or 8-bit extended-ASCII coding system would be short-sighted in view of development towards 16-bit and 32-bit processors. In fact, any specific recommendations would tie the Association to a stage of technological development which is bound to be outdated long before the next revision of the handbook.

The coding convention was not meant to address the engineering aspects of the actual encoding in computers (cf. Anderson (1984)). However, it was meant to serve as a basis for a interchange standard for creating mapping tables from various computer encodings, fonts, phonetic-character-set software, etc., to common IPA numbers, and therefore symbols.[6]

Furthermore, the assignment of computer codes to IPA symbols was meant to represent an unbiased formulation. The Association here played the role of an international advisory body and it stated that it should not recommend a particular existing system of encoding. In fact, during this time there were a number of coding systems used (see Section 1.2), but none of them had a dominant international position. The differences between systems were also either too great or too subtle to warrant an attempt at combining them (Roach 1989).

The working group assigned each IPA symbol to a unique three-digit IPA number. Encoded in this number scheme implicitly is information about the status of each symbol (see below). The IPA numbers were listed with the IPA symbols and they were also illustrated in IPA chart form (see Esling & Gaylord (1993: 84) or The International Phonetic Association (1999: App. 2)). The numbers were assigned in linear order (e.g. [p] 101, [b] 102, [t] 103...) following the IPA revision of 1989 and its update in 1996. Although the numbering scheme still exists, in practice it is superseded by the Unicode codification of symbols.

[6]Remember, at this time in the late 1980s there was no stable multilingual computing environment. But some solution was needed because scholars were increasingly using personal computers for their research and many were quickly adopting electronic mail or discussion boards like Usenet as a medium for international exchanges. Most of these systems ran on 8-bit hardware systems using a 7-bit ASCII character encoding.

The working group made the decision that no IPA symbol, past or present, could be ignored. The comprehensive inclusion of all IPA symbols was to anticipate the possibility that some symbols might be added, withdrawn, or reintroduced into current or future usage. For example, in the 1989 revision voiceless implosives < ƥ, ƭ, ƈ, ƙ, ʠ > were added; in the 1993 revision they were removed. Ligatures like < ʧ, ʤ > are included as formerly recognized IPA symbols; they are assigned to the 200 series of IPA numbers as members of the group of symbols formerly recognized by the IPA. To ensure backwards compatibility, legacy IPA symbols would retain an IPA number and an IPA name for reference purposes. As we discuss below, this decision is later reflected in the Unicode Standard as many legacy IPA symbols still reside in the IPA Extensions block.

The IPA number is expressed as a three-digit number. The first digit indicates the symbol's category (Esling 1990; Esling & Gaylord 1993):

- 100s for accepted IPA consonants
- 200s for former IPA consonants and non-IPA symbols
- 300s for vowels
- 400s for segmental diacritics
- 500s for suprasegmental symbols
- 600s-800s for future specifications
- 900s for escape sequences

After a symbol is categorized, it is assigned a number sequentially, e.g. [i] 301, [e] 302, [ɛ] 303. The system allows for the addition of new symbols within the various series by appending them, e.g. [ⱱ] 184. Former non-IPA symbols (or often-used but non-official IPA symbols) for consonants, vowels and diacritics are numbered from 299 backwards. For example, the voiceless and voiced postalveolar affricates and fricatives < č, ǰ, š, ž > are assigned the IPA numbers 299, 298, 297 and 296, respectively, because they are not sanctioned IPA symbols.

The assignment of the IPA numbers to IPA symbols provided the basis for uniquely identifying the set of past and present IPA symbols as a type of computational representational standard of the IPA. Within each revision of the IPA, the coding defines a closed and clearly defined set of characters. The benefits of this standardization are clear in at least two ways: it is used in translation tables that reference ASCII representations of the IPA, and this early computational representation of the IPA became the basis for X-SAMPA and for the inclusion of the IPA into the Unicode Standard version 1.0.

SAMPA and X-SAMPA

True to the working group's aim, the IPA numbers provided a mechanism for an interchange standard for creating mapping tables to various computer encodings. For example, the IPA coding system was used as a mapping system in the creation of SAMPA (Wells et al. 1992), an ASCII representation of the IPA symbols.

For a long time, linguists, like all other computer users, were limited to ASCII-encoded 7-bit characters, which only includes Latin characters, numbers and some punctuation and symbols. Restricted to these standard character sets that lacked IPA support or other language-specific graphemes that they needed, linguists devised their own solutions.[7] For example, some chose to represent unavailable graphemes with substitutes, e.g. the combination of <ng> to represent <ŋ>. Tech-savvy linguists redefined selected characters from a character encoding by mapping custom-made fonts to specific code points.[8] However, one linguist's electronic text would not render properly on another linguist's computer without access to the same font. Furthermore, if two character encodings defined two character sets differently, then data could not be reliably and correctly displayed. This is a commonly encountered example of the non-interoperability of data and data formats.

One solution was the ASCII-ification of the IPA, which simply involved defining keyboard-able sequences consisting of ASCII combinations as IPA symbols. For example, Wells (1987) provides an in-depth description of IPA codings from country-to-country. Later ASCII-IPAs include Kirshenbaum (created in 1992 in a Usenet group and named after its lead developer who was at Hewlett-Packard Laboratories) and Worldbet (published by Hieronymus (1993), who was at AT&T Laboratories). The most successful effort was SAMPA (Speech Assessment Methods Phonetic Alphabet), which was created between 1988–1991 in Europe to represent IPA symbols with ASCII character sequences (Wells 1987; Wells et al. 1992), using e.g. <p\> for [ɸ]. SAMPA was developed by a group of speech scientists from nine countries in Europe and it constituted the ASCII-IPA symbols needed for phonemic transcription of the principal European languages (Wells 1995). It is still widely used in language technology.

Two problems with SAMPA are that (i) it is only a partial encoding of the IPA and (ii) it encodes different languages in separate data tables, instead of using

[7] Early work addressing the need for a universal computing environment for writing systems and their computational complexity is discussed in Simons (1989). A more recent survey of practical recommendations for language resources, including notes on encoding, can be found in Bird & Simons (2003).

[8] For example, SIL's popular font SIL IPA 1990.

a universal alphabet, like IPA. SAMPA tables were developed as part of a European Commission-funded project to address technical problems like electronic mail exchange (what is now simply called email). SAMPA is essentially a hack to work around displaying IPA characters, but it provided speech technology and other fields a basis that has been widely adopted and often still used in code. So, SAMPA is a collection of tables to be compared, instead of a large universal table representing all languages.

An extended version of SAMPA, called X-SAMPA, set out to include every symbol, including all diacritics, in the IPA chart (Wells 1995). X-SAMPA is considered more universally applicable because it consists of one table that encodes all characters in IPA. In line with the principles of the IPA, SAMPA and X-SAMPA include a repertoire of symbols. These symbols are intended to represent phonemes rather than all allophonic distinctions. Additionally, both ASCII-ifications of IPA – SAMPA and X-SAMPA – are (reportedly) uniquely parsable (Wells 1995). However, like the IPA, X-SAMPA has different notations for encoding the same phonetic phenomena (cf. Section 5.5).

SAMPA and X-SAMPA have been widely used for speech technology and as an encoding system in computational linguistics. In fact, they are still used in popular software packages that require ASCII input, e.g. RuG/L04 and SplitsTree4.[9]

4.4 The need for a single multilingual environment

In hindsight it is easy to lose sight of how impactful 30 years of technological development have been on linguistics, from theory development using quantitative means to pure data collection and dissemination. But at the end of the 1970s, virtually no ordinary working linguist was using a personal computer (Simons 1996). Personal computer usage, however, dramatically increased throughout the 1980s. By 1990, dozens of character sets were in common use. They varied in their architecture and in their character repertoires, which made things a mess.

During the 1980s, it became increasingly clear that an adequate solution to the problem of multilingual computing environments was needed. Linguists were on the forefront of addressing this issue because they faced these challenges head-on by wishing to publish and communicate electronic text with phonetic symbols which were not included in basic ASCII. One only needs to look at facsimiles of older electronic documents to see exotic symbols written in by hand after the preparation of typed version.

[9] See http://www.let.rug.nl/kleiweg/L04/ and http://www.splitstree.org/, respectively.

A major benefit of the standardization of the IPA in a computational representation by the Kiel working group is that it provided the basis for a formal proposal to be submitted to various international standards organizations, several of which were trying to tackle (and in a sense win) the multilingual computing environment problem (cf. Section 1.2). Basically, everyone – from corporations to governments to language scientists – wanted a single unified multilingual character encoding set for all the world's writing systems, even if they did not understand or appreciate the challenges involved in creating and adopting a solution.

Industry was starting to tackle the issues involved in developing a single multilingual computing environment on a variety of fronts, including the then new technology of bitmap fonts and the creation of Font Manager and Script Manager by Apple (Apple Computer 1985; 1986; 1988). As noted above, around this time linguists were developing work-arounds such as SAMPA, so that they could communicate IPA transcription and use ASCII-based software. Some linguists formalized the issues of multilingual text processing from a computational perspective (Anderson 1984; Becker 1984; Simons 1989). The study of writing systems was also being invigorated (Sampson 1985: 11–15) by the computational challenges in making computers work in a multilingual environment. The engineering problems and solutions had been spelled out years before, e.g. a two-byte encoding for multilingual text (Anderson 1984). Although languages vary to an astounding extent (cf. Evans & Levinson (2009)), writing systems are quite similar formally and the issue of formal representation of the world's orthographic systems had already been addressed (Simons 1989).

After the Kiel Convention in 1989, the working group assisted the International Phonetic Association in representing the IPA to the INTERNATIONAL ORGANIZATION FOR STANDARDIZATION (ISO) and to the TEXT ENCODING INITIATIVE (TEI) (Esling & Gaylord 1993). The working group's formalization of the IPA, i.e. a full listing of agreed-upon computer codings for phonetic symbols, was used in developing writing system descriptions, which were at the time being solicited for scripts to be included in the new multilingual international character encoding standards. The working group for ISO/IEC 10646 and Unicode were two such initiatives.

In the historical context of the IPA being considered for inclusion in ISO/IEC 10646, it is important to realize that there were a variety of sources (i.e. not just from the Association) which submitted character proposals for phonetic alphabets. These proposals, including the one from the Association via the Kiel working group, were considered as a whole by the ISO working groups that were responsible for incorporating a phonetic script into the universal character set

(UCS). The ISO working groups that were responsible for assigning a phonetic character set then made their own submissions as part of a review process by ISO for approval based on both informatics and phonetic criteria (Esling & Gaylord 1993: 86).

Character set ISO/IEC 10646 was approved by ISO, including the phonetic characters submitted to them in May 1993. The set of IPA characters were assigned UCS codes in 16-bit representation (in hexadecimal) and were published as Tables 2 and 3 in Esling & Gaylord (1993), which include a graphical representation of the IPA symbol, its IPA name, phonetic description, IPA number, UCS code and AFII code.[10] When the character sets of ISO/IEC 10646 and the Unicode Standard later converged (see Chapter 2), the IPA proposal was included in the Unicode Standard Version 1.0 – largely as we know it today.

With subsequent revisions to the IPA, one might have expected that the Unicode Consortium would update the Unicode Standard in a way that is in line with the development of linguistic insights. However, updates that go against the principle of maintaining backwards compatibility lose out, i.e. it is more important to deal with the pitfalls created along the way than it is to change the standard. Therefore, many of the pitfalls we encounter today when using Unicode IPA are historic relics that we have to come to grips with.

It was a long journey, but the goal of achieving a single multilingual computing environment has largely been accomplished. As such, we should not dismiss the IPA numbers or pre-Unicode encoding attempts, such as SAMPA/X-SAMPA, as misguided. The parallels between the IPA numbers and Unicode Code points, for example, are striking because both the IPA and the Unicode Consortium came up with the solution of an additional layer of indirection (an abstraction layer) between symbols/characters and encoding on the bit pattern level. SAMPA/X-SAMPA is also still useful as an input method for IPA in ASCII and required by some software.

Current users of the Unicode Standard must cope with the pitfalls that were dug along the way, as will be discussed in the next chapter. As the Association foresightfully remarked about Unicode:

> *"When this character set is in wide use,*
> *it will be the normal way to encode IPA symbols."*
>
> (The International Phonetic Association 1999: 164).

[10] The Association for Font Information Interchange (AFII) was an international database of glyphs created to promote the standardization of font data required to produce ISO/IEC 10646.

5 IPA meets Unicode

5.1 The twain shall meet

The International Phonetic Alphabet (IPA) is a common standard in linguistics to transcribe sounds of spoken language into discrete segments using a Latin-based alphabet. Although IPA is reasonably easily adhered to with pen and paper, it is not trivial to encode IPA characters electronically. In this chapter we discuss various pitfalls with the encoding of IPA in the Unicode Standard. We will specifically refer to the 2015 version of the IPA (The International Phonetic Association 2015) and the 11.0.0 version of Unicode (The Unicode Consortium 2018).

As long as a transcription is only directed towards phonetically trained eyes, then all the details of the Unicode-encoding are unimportant. For a linguist reading an IPA transcription, many of the details that will be discussed in this chapter might seem like hair-splitting trivialities. However, if IPA transcriptions are intended to be used across resources (e.g. searching similar phenomena across different languages) then it becomes crucial that there are strict encoding guidelines. Our main goal in this chapter is to present the encoding issues and propose recommendations for a strict IPA encoding for situations in which cross-resource consistency is crucial.

There are several pitfalls to be aware of when using the Unicode Standard to encode IPA. As we have said before, from a linguistic perspective it might sometimes look like the Unicode Consortium is making incomprehensible decisions, but it is important to realize that the consortium has tried and is continuing to try to be as consistent as possible across a wide range of use cases, and it does place linguistic traditions above other orthographic choices. Furthermore, when we look at the history of how the IPA met Unicode, we see that many of the decisions for IPA symbols in the Unicode Standard come directly from the International Phonetic Association itself. Therefore, many pitfalls that we will encounter have their grounding in the history of the principles of the IPA, as well as in the technological considerations involved in creating a single multilingual encoding. In general, we strongly suggest to linguists to not complain about any decisions in the Unicode Standard, but to try and understand the rationale of the

International Phonetic Association and the Unicode Consortium (both of which are almost always well-conceived in our experience) and devise ways to work with any unexpected behavior.

Many of the current problems derive from the fact that the IPA is clearly historically based on the Latin script, but different enough from most other Latin-based writing systems to warrant special attention. This ambivalent status of the IPA glyphs (partly Latin, partly special) is unfortunately also attested in the treatment of IPA in the Unicode Standard. In retrospect, it might have been better to consider the IPA (and other transcription systems) to be a special kind of script within the Unicode Standard, and treat the obvious similarity to Latin glyphs as a historical relic. All IPA glyphs would then have their own code points, instead of the current situation in which some IPA glyphs have special code points, while others are treated as being identical to the regular Latin characters. Yet, the current situation, however unfortunate, is unlikely to change, so as linguists we must learn to deal with the specific pitfalls of IPA within the Unicode Standard.

5.2 Pitfall: No complete IPA code block

The ambivalent nature of IPA glyphs arises because, on the one hand, the IPA uses Latin-based glyphs like <a>, <b> or <p>. From this perspective, the IPA seems to be just another orthographic tradition using Latin characters, all of which do not get a special treatment within the Unicode Standard (just like e.g. the French, German, or Danish orthographic traditions do not have a special status). On the other hand, the IPA uses many special symbols (like turned <ɐ>, mirrored <ɘ> and/or extended <ɧ> Latin glyphs) not found in any other Latin-based writing system. For this reason a special block with code points, called IPA Extensions was already included in the first version of the Unicode Standard (Version 1.0 from 1991).

As explained in Section 3.6, the Unicode Standard code space is subdivided into character blocks, which generally encode characters from a single script. However, as is illustrated by the IPA, characters that form a single writing system may be dispersed across several different character blocks. With its diverse collection of symbols from various scripts and diacritics, the IPA is spread across 12 blocks in the Unicode Standard:[1]

[1] This number of blocks depends on whether only IPA-sanctioned symbols are counted or if the phonetic symbols commonly found in the literature are also included, see Moran (2012: Appendix C). The 159 characters from 12 code blocks shown here are the characters proposed for strict IPA encoding, as discussed in Section 5.13.

- Basic Latin (27 characters)
  a b c d e f h i j k l m n o p q r s t u v w x y z . |
- Latin-1 Supplement (4 characters)
  æ ç ð ø
- Latin Extended-A (3 characters)
  ħ ŋ œ
- Latin Extended-B (4 characters)
  ǀ ǁ ǂ ǃ
- Latin Extended-C (1 character):
  ⱱ
- IPA Extensions (67 characters)
  ɐ ɑ ɒ ɓ ɔ ɕ ɖ ɗ ɘ ə ɛ ɜ ɞ ɟ ɠ ɡ ɢ ɣ ɤ ɥ ɦ ɧ ɨ ɪ ɬ ɭ ɮ ɯ ɰ ɱ ɲ ɳ ɴ
  ɵ ɶ ɸ ɹ ɺ ɻ ɽ ɾ ʀ ʁ ʂ ʃ ʄ ʈ ʉ ʊ ʋ ʌ ʍ ʎ ʏ ʐ ʑ ʒ ʔ ʕ ʘ ʙ ʛ ʜ ʝ ʟ ʡ ʢ
- Greek and Coptic (3 characters)
  β θ χ
- Spacing Modifier Letters (17 characters)
  ◌˞ ◌ˡ ◌ʷ ◌ʲ ◌ˠ ◌ˤ ◌ʰ ◌ʼ ◌ː ◌ˑ ˥ ˦ ˧ ˨ ˩ ˈ ˌ
- Superscripts and Subscripts (1 character)
  ◌ⁿ
- Combining Diacritical Marks (25 characters)
  ◌̼ ◌̺ ◌̻ ◌̪ ◌̟ ◌̠ ◌̝ ◌̞ ◌̘ ◌̙ ◌̜ ◌̹ ◌̬ ◌̥ ◌̰ ◌̤ ◌̩ ◌̯ ◌̴ ◌̃ ◌̈ ◌̽ ◌̆ ◌̚ ◌͡◌
- General Punctuation (2 characters)
  ‖ ‿
- Arrows (4 characters)
  ↑ ↓ ↗ ↘

5.3 Pitfall: IPA homoglyphs in Unicode

Another problem is the large number of homoglyphs, i.e. different characters that have highly similar glyphs (or even completely identical glyphs, depending on the font rendering). For example, a user of a Cyrillic computer keyboard should ideally not use the <а> CYRILLIC SMALL LETTER A at code point U+0430 for IPA transcriptions, but instead use the <a> LATIN SMALL LETTER A at code point U+0061, although visually they are mostly indistinguishable, and the Cyrillic character is more easily typed on a Cyrillic keyboard. Some further problematic homoglyphs related to encoding IPA in the Unicode Standard are the following:

- The uses of the apostrophe have led to long discussions on the Unicode Standard email list. An English keyboard inputs the symbol <◌'> APOSTROPHE at U+0027, although the preferred Unicode apostrophe is the <◌’> RIGHT SINGLE QUOTATION MARK at U+2019.[2] However, the glottal stop/glottalization/ejective marker is yet another completely different character, namely <◌ʼ>, i.e. the MODIFIER LETTER APOSTROPHE at U+02BC, which unfortunately looks extremely similar to U+2019.
- Another problem is the <◌ˁ> MODIFIER LETTER REVERSED GLOTTAL STOP at U+02C1 vs. the <◌ˤ> MODIFIER LETTER SMALL REVERSED GLOTTAL STOP at U+02E4. Both appear in various resources representing phonetic data online. This is thus a clear example for which the Unicode Standard does not solve the linguistic standardization problem.
- Linguists are also unlikely to distinguish between the <ə> LATIN SMALL LETTER SCHWA at code point U+0259 and <ǝ> LATIN SMALL LETTER TURNED E at U+01DD.
- The alveolar click <ǃ> at U+01C3 is of course often simply typed as <!> EXCLAMATION MARK at U+0021.[3]
- The dental click <ǀ>, in Unicode known as LATIN LETTER DENTAL CLICK at U+01C0, is often simply typed as <|> VERTICAL LINE at U+007C.
- For the marking of length there is a special Unicode character, namely <◌ː> MODIFIER LETTER TRIANGULAR COLON at U+02D0. However, typing <◌:> COLON at U+003A is of course much easier.
- There are two mostly identical-looking Unicode characters for the superscript <ʰ>: the COMBINING LATIN SMALL LETTER H at U+036A and the MODIFIER LETTER SMALL H at U+02B0. Making the situation even more problematic is that they have different behavior (see Section 5.9). To harmonize the behavior of <ʰ> with other superscript letters, we propose to standardize on the modifier letter at U+02B0 (see Section 5.10).

Conversely, non-linguists are unlikely to distinguish any semantic difference between an open back unrounded vowel, which is encoded in IPA with a “single-story” <ɑ> LATIN SMALL LETTER ALPHA at U+0251, and the open front unrounded

[2] Note that many word processors (like Microsoft Word) by default will replace straight quotes by curly quotes, depending on the whitespace around it.

[3] In the Unicode Standard the <ǃ> at U+01C3 is labeled LATIN LETTER RETROFLEX CLICK, but in IPA that glyph is used for an alveolar or postalveolar click (not retroflex). This naming is probably best seen as an error in the Unicode Standard. For the real retroflex click, see Section 5.12.

vowel, which is encoded in IPA with a "double-story" <a> LATIN SMALL LETTER A at U+0061, basically treating them as homoglyphs, although they are different phonetic symbols. But even among linguists this distinction leads to problems. For example, as pointed out by Mielke (2009), there is a problem stemming from the fact that about 75% of languages are reported to have a five-vowel system (Maddieson 1984). Historically, linguistic descriptions tend not to include precise audio recording and measurements of formants, so this may lead one to ask if the many <a> characters that are used in phonological description reflects a transcriptional bias. The common use of <a> in transcriptions could be in part due to the ease of typing the letter on an English keyboard (or for older descriptions, the typewriter). We found it to be exceedingly rare that a linguist uses <ɑ> for a low back unrounded vowel.[4] They simply use <a> as long as there is no opposition to <ɑ>.

Making things even more problematic, there is an old typographic tradition that the double-story <a> uses a single-story <ɑ> in italics. This leads to the unfortunate effect that even in many well-designed fonts the italics of <a> and <ɑ> use the same glyph. For example, in Linux Libertine (the font of this book) the italics of these characters are highly similar, <*a*> and <*ɑ*>, while in Charis SIL they are identical: <*a*> and <*ɑ*>. If this distinction has to be kept upright in italics, the only solution we can currently offer is to use SLANTED glyphs (i.e. artificially italicized glyphs) instead of real italics (i.e. special italics glyphs designed by a typographer).[5] This approach was taken by the Language Science Press to

[4] One example is Vidal (2001: 75), in which the author states: "The definition of Pilagá /a/ as [+back] results from its behavior in certain phonological contexts. For instance, uvular and pharyngeal consonants only occur around /a/ and /o/. Hence, the characterization of /a/ and /o/ as a natural class of (i.e. [+back] vowels), as opposed to /i/ and /e/."

[5] For example, the widely used IPA font Doulos SIL (https://software.sil.org/doulos/) does not have real italics. This leads some word-processing software, like Microsoft Word, to produce slanted glyphs instead. That particular combination of font and software application will thus lead to the desired effect distinguishing <a> from <ɑ> in italics. However, note that when the text is transferred to another font (i.e. one that includes real italics) and/or to another software application (like Apple Pages, which does not perform slanting), then this visual appearance will be lost. In this case we are thus still in the pre-Unicode situation in which the choice of font and rendering software actually matters. The ideal solution from a linguistic point of view would be the introduction of a new IPA code point for a different kind of <a>, which explicitly specifies that it should still be rendered as a double-story character when italicized. After informal discussion with various Unicode players, our impression is that this highly restricted problem is not sufficiently urgent to introduce even more <a> homographs in Unicode (which already lead to much confusion, see Section 3.8).

distinguish between the two different orthographic <a>'s in Chakali in Brindle (2017).[6]

Lastly, before we move on from the pitfall of IPA homoglyphs in Unicode to the pitfall of homoglyphs in IPA, we are aware of one example that illustrates both pitfalls. Consider for example what one reviewer coined i dot-suppression. When combining, say the latin small letter i <i> at U+0069 with the combining acute accent <◌́> at U+0301, the result is the combination of these two characters into <í> or the associated precomposed form latin small letter i with acute <í> at U+00ED. Typographically, the accent mark replaces the dot. In IPA, the <í> denotes a high front unrounded vowel with high tone. However, the result of losing the dot makes this IPA symbol look very similar to the near-high near-front unrounded vowel <ɪ>, when it also has the high tone marker: <ɪ́>. To boot, when an accent mark is added to latin small letter i with stroke <ɨ> at U+0268, the dot is not suppressed but retained, i.e. <ɨ́>.[7]

5.4 Pitfall: Homoglyphs in IPA

Reversely, there are a few cases in which the IPA distinguishes different phonetic concepts, but the visual characters used by the IPA look very much alike. Such cases are thus homoglyphs in the IPA itself, which of course need different encodings.

- The dental click <ǀ> and the indication of a minor group break <|> look almost the same in most fonts. For a proper encoding, the latin letter dental click at U+01C0 and the vertical line at U+007C should be used, respectively.
- Similarly, the alveolar lateral click <ǁ> should be encoded with a latin letter lateral click at U+01C1, different from <‖>, which according to the IPA is the character to by used for a major group break (by intonation), to be encoded by double vertical line at U+2016.
- The marking of primary stress < ˈ > looks like an apostrophe, and is often typed with the same symbol as the ejective <◌’>. For a proper encoding, these two symbols should be typed as modifier letter vertical line at U+02C8 and modifier letter apostrophe at U+02BC, respectively.

[6] http://langsci-press.org/catalog/book/74

[7] According to the Unicode Standard, latin small letter i with stroke <ɨ> at U+0268 cannot be decomposed into, say, latin small letter i <i> at U+0069 and combining short stroke overlay <◌̵> at U+0335. We discuss the pitfall of missing decomposition forms in Section 5.8.

- There are two different dashed-l characters in IPA, namely the <ɫ> LATIN SMALL LETTER L WITH MIDDLE TILDE at U+026B and the <ɬ> LATIN SMALL LETTER L WITH BELT at U+026C. These of course look highly similar, although they are different sounds. As a solution, we will actually propose to not use the middle tilde at all (see Section 5.5).

5.5 Pitfall: Multiple encoding options in IPA

It is not just the Unicode Standard that offers multiple options for encoding the IPA. Even the IPA specification itself offers some flexibility in how transcriptions have to be encoded. There are a few cases in which the IPA explicitly allows for different options of transcribing the same phonetic content. This is understandable from a transcriber's point of view, but it is not acceptable when the goal is interoperability between resources written in IPA. We consider it crucial to distinguish between valid IPA, for which it is sufficient that any phonetically-trained reader is able to understand the transcription, and strict IPA, which should be standardized on a single unique encoding for each sound, so search will work across resources. We are aware of the following non-unique encoding options in the IPA, which will be discussed in turn below:

- The marking of tone
- The marking of <g>
- The marking of velarization and pharyngealization
- The placement of diacritics

The first case in which the IPA allows for different encodings is the question of how to transcribe tone (cf. Maddieson (1990)). There is an old tradition to use diacritics on vowels to mark different tone levels (The International Phonetic Association 1949). Prior to the 1989 Kiel convention, IPA-approved tone symbols included diacritics above or below the vowel or syllable, e.g. high and low tones marked with macrons (<◌̄>, <◌̱>), and acute and grave accents for high rising tone <◌́>, low rising tone <◌̗>, high falling tone <◌̀> and low falling tone <◌̖>. These tone symbols, however, had failed to catch on (probably) due to aesthetic objections and matters of adequacy for transcription (Maddieson 1990: 29).

After the 1989 Kiel convention, the accent tone symbols were updated to the tradition that we are familiar with today and which was already in wide use by Africanists and others, namely level tones <◌̋, ◌́, ◌̄, ◌̀, ◌̏> and contour tones

<◌̌, ◌̂, ◌᷄, ◌᷅, ◌᷈>.[8] In addition, the IPA also adopted tone letters developed by Chao (1930), e.g. <˥˥˧˨˩>, which were in wide use by Asianists.[9] Tone letters in the IPA have five different levels, and sequences of these letters can be used to indicate contours. Well-designed fonts will even merge a sequence of tone letters into a contour. For example, compare the font Linux Libertine, which does not merge tone letters <˥˩˧˩>, with the font CharisSIL, which merges this sequence of four tone letters into a single contour <˥˩˧˩>. For strict IPA encoding we propose to standardize on tone letters.

Second, we commonly encounter the use of <g> LATIN SMALL LETTER G at U+0067, instead of the Unicode Standard IPA character for the voiced velar stop <ɡ> LATIN SMALL LETTER SCRIPT G at U+0261. One begins to question whether this issue is at all apparent to the working linguist, or if they simply use the U+0067 because it is easily keyboarded and thus saves time, whereas the latter must be cumbersomely inserted as a special symbol in most software. The International Phonetic Association has taken the stance that both the keyboard LATIN SMALL LETTER G and the LATIN SMALL LETTER SCRIPT G are valid input characters for the voiced velar plosive (The International Phonetic Association 1999: 19).[10] Unfortunately, this decision further introduces ambiguity for linguists trying to adhere to a strict Unicode Standard IPA encoding. For strict IPA encoding we propose to standardize on the more idiosyncratic LATIN SMALL LETTER SCRIPT G at U+0261.

Third, the IPA has special markers for velarization <◌ˠ> and pharyngealization <◌ˤ>. Confusingly, there is also a marker for "velarized or pharyngealized", using the <◌̴> COMBINING TILDE OVERLAY at U+0334. The tilde overlay seems to be extremely rarely used. We suggest to try and avoid using the tilde overlay, though for reasons of backward compatibility we will allow it in valid-IPA.

Finally, the IPA states that "diacritics may be placed above a symbol with a descender". For example, for marking of voiceless pronunciation of voiced segments the IPA uses the ring diacritic. Originally, the ring should be placed below the

[8]To make things even more complicated, there are at least two different Unicode homoglyphs for the low and high level tones, namely <◌̀> COMBINING GRAVE TONE MARK at U+0340 vs. <◌̀> COMBINING GRAVE ACCENT at U+0300 for low tone, and <◌́> COMBINING ACUTE TONE MARK at U+0341 vs.<◌́> COMBINING ACUTE ACCENT at U+0301 for high tone.

[9]Not sanctioned by the IPA, but nevertheless widely attested, is the use of superscript numbers for marking tones, also proposed by Chao (1930). One issue to note here is that superscript numbers can be either regular numbers that are formatted as superscript with a text processor, or they can be separate superscript characters, as defined in the Unicode Standard (see: https://en.wikipedia.org/wiki/Superscripts_and_Subscripts). This divide means that searching text is dependent on how the author formatted or encoded the superscript numbers.

[10]Note however that the current instructions for contributors to the Journal of the International Phonetic Association requires the use of opentail <ɡ> and not looptail <g>.

base character, like in <m̥>, using the COMBINING RING BELOW at U+0325. However, in letters with long descenders the IPA also allows to put the ring above the base, like in <ŋ̊>, using the COMBINING RING ABOVE at U+030A. Yet, proper font design does not have any problem with rendering the ring below the base character, like in <ŋ̥>, so for strict IPA encoding we propose to standardize on the ring below. As a principle, for strict IPA encoding only one option should be allowed for all diacritics.

The variable encoding as allowed by the IPA becomes even more troublesome for the tilde and diaeresis diacritics. In these cases, the IPA itself attaches different semantics to the symbols above and below a base characters. The tilde above a character (like in <ã>, using the COMBINING TILDE at U+0303) is used for nasalization, while the tilde below a character (like in <a̰>, using the COMBINING TILDE BELOW at U+0330) indicates creaky voice. Likewise, the diaeresis above (like in <ä>, using the COMBINING DIAERESIS at U+0308) is used for centralization, while the diaeresis below a character (like in <a̤>, using the COMBINING DIAERESIS BELOW at U+0324) indicates breathy voice. These cases strengthen our plea to not allow diacritics to switch position for typographic convenience.

5.6 Pitfall: Tie bar

In the major revision of the IPA in 1932, affricates were represented by two consonants <tʃ>, ligatures <ʧ>, or with the tie bar <t͡ʃ>. In the 1938 revision the tie bar's semantics were broadened to indicate simultaneous articulation, as for example in labial velars such as <k͡p>. Thus, the tie bar is a convenient diacritic for visually tokenizing input strings into chunks of phonetically salient groups, including affricates, doubly articulated consonants or diphthongs.

The tie bar can be placed above or below the base characters, e.g. <t͡s> or <t͜s>. IPA allows both options. The choice between the two symbols is purely for legible rendering; there is no difference in semantics between the two symbols. However, rendering is such a problematic issue for tie bars in general that many linguists simply do not use them. Just looking at a few different fonts already indicates that actually no font designer really gets the placement right in combination with superscripts and subscripts. If really necessary, we propose to standardize on the tie bar above the base characters, using a COMBINING DOUBLE INVERTED BREVE at U+0361.[11]

[11] Also note that the UNDERTIE at U+203F looks like the tie bar below and is easily confused with it. However, it is a different character and has a different function in IPA. The undertie is

Times new Roman: t̥ʰ͡s t̥ʰ͜s

CharisSIL: t̥ʰ͡s t̥ʰ͜s

Monaco: t̥ʰ͡s t̥ʰ͜s

DoulosSIL: t̥ʰ͡s t̥ʰ͜s

Linux Libertine: t̥ʰ͡s t̥ʰ͜s

Tie bars are a special type of character in the sense that they do not belong to a segment, but bind two graphemes together. This actually turns out to be rather different from Unicode conceptions. The Unicode encoding of this character belong to the Combining Diacritical Marks, namely either COMBINING DOUBLE INVERTED BREVE at U+0361 or COMBINING DOUBLE BREVE BELOW at U+035C. Such a combining mark is by definition tied to the character in front, but not the character following it. The Unicode treatment of this character thus only partly corresponds to the IPA conception, which ideally would have the tie bar linked both to the character in front and to the character following.

Further, according to the spirit of the IPA, it would also be possible to combine more than two base characters into one tie bar, but this is not possible with Unicode (i.e. there is no possibility to draw a tie bar over three or four characters). It is possible to indicate such larger groups by repeating the tie bar, like for a triphthong <a͡ʊ͡ə> in the English word *hour*. If really necessary, we consider this possible, even though the rendering will never look good.

Most importantly though, in comparison to normal Unicode processing, the tie bar actually takes a reversed approach to complex graphemes. Basically, the Unicode principle (see Section 3.3) is that fixed sequences in a writing system have to be specified as tailored grapheme clusters. Only in case the sequence is not a cluster, then this has to be explicitly indicated. IPA takes a different approach. In IPA by default different base letters are not connected into larger clusters; only when it is specified in the string itself (using the tie bar).

5.7 Pitfall: Ligatures and digraphs

One important distinction to acknowledge is the difference between multigraphs and ligatures. Multigraphs are groups of characters (in the context of IPA e.g. <tʃ> or <ou>) while ligatures are single characters (e.g. <ʧ> LATIN SMALL LETTER TESH

used as a linking symbol to indicate the lack of a boundary, e.g. French *petit ami* [pətit‿ami] 'boyfriend'.

DIGRAPH at U+02A7). Ligatures arose in the context of printing easier-to-read texts, and are included in the Unicode Standard for reasons of legacy encoding. However, their usage is discouraged by the Unicode core specification. Specifically related to IPA, various phonetic combinations of characters (typically affricates) are available as single code points in the Unicode Standard, but are designated DIGRAPHS. Such glyphs might be used by software to produce a pleasing display, but they should not be hard-coded into the text itself. In the context of IPA, characters like the following ligatures should thus *not* be used. Instead a combination of two characters is preferred:

<ʣ> LATIN SMALL LETTER DZ DIGRAPH at U+02A3 (use <dz>)
<ʤ> LATIN SMALL LETTER DEZH DIGRAPH at U+02A4 (use <dʒ>)
<ʥ> LATIN SMALL LETTER DZ DIGRAPH WITH CURL at U+02A5 (use <dʑ>)
<ʦ> LATIN SMALL LETTER TS DIGRAPH at U+02A6 (use <ts>)
<ʧ> LATIN SMALL LETTER TESH DIGRAPH at U+02A7 (use <tʃ>)
<ʨ> LATIN SMALL LETTER TC DIGRAPH WITH CURL at U+02A8 (use <tɕ>)
<ʩ> LATIN SMALL LETTER FENG DIGRAPH at U+02A9 (use <fŋ>)

However, there are a few Unicode characters that are historically ligatures, but which are today considered as simple characters in the Unicode Standard and thus should be used when writing IPA, namely:

<ɮ> LATIN SMALL LETTER LEZH at U+026E
<œ> LATIN SMALL LIGATURE OE at U+0153
<ɶ> LATIN LETTER SMALL CAPITAL OE at U+0276
<æ> LATIN SMALL LETTER AE at U+00E6

5.8 Pitfall: Missing decomposition

Although many combinations of base character with diacritic are treated as with precomposed characters, there are a few combinations in IPA that allow for multiple, apparently identical, encodings that are not (see Section 3.9 on the principle of canonical equivalence). For that reason, the following elements should not be treated as diacritics when encoding IPA in Unicode:

<◌̡> COMBINING PALATALIZED HOOK BELOW at U+0321
<◌̢> COMBINING RETROFLEX HOOK BELOW at U+0322
<◌̵> COMBINING SHORT STROKE OVERLAY at U+0335
<◌̷> COMBINING SHORT SOLIDUS OVERLAY at U+0337

There turn out to be a lot of characters in the IPA that could be conceived as using any of these elements, like <ɲ>, <ɳ>, <ɨ> or <ø>. However, all such characters exist as well as precomposed combination in Unicode, and these precomposed characters should preferably be used. When combinations of a base character with diacritic are used instead, then these combinations are not to the precomposed combinations. This means that any search will not find both at the same time.

A similar problem arises with the rhotic hook. There are two precomposed characters in Unicode with a rhotic hook, which are not with a combination of the vowel with a separately encoded hook:

<ɚ> LATIN SMALL LETTER SCHWA WITH HOOK at U+025A
<ɝ> LATIN SMALL LETTER REVERSED OPEN E WITH HOOK at U+025D

All other combinations of vowels with rhotic hooks will have to be made by using <◌˞> MODIFIER LETTER RHOTIC HOOK at U+02DE, because there is no complete set of precomposed characters with rhotic hooks in Unicode. For that reason we propose to not use the two precomposed characters with hooks mentioned above, but always use the separate rhotic hook at U+02DE in IPA.

A similar situation arises with <◌̴> COMBINING TILDE OVERLAY at U+0334. The main reason some phoneticians like to use this in IPA is to mark the dark <l> in English codas, using the character <ɫ> LATIN SMALL LETTER L WITH MIDDLE TILDE at U+026B. This character is not canonically equivalent to the combination <l> + <◌̴>, so one of the two possible encodings has to be chosen. Because the tilde overlay is described as a general mechanism by the IPA, we propose to use the separated <◌̴> COMBINING TILDE OVERLAY at U+0334. However, note that phonetically this seems to be (almost) superfluous (see Section 5.5) and the typical usage in the form of <ɫ> is (almost) a homoglyph with <ɬ> (see Section 5.4). For these reasons we also suggest to try and avoid the tilde overlay completely.

Reversely, note that the <ç> LATIN SMALL LETTER C WITH CEDILLA at U+00E7 is with <c> with <◌̧> COMBINING CEDILLA at U+0327, so it will be separated into two characters by Unicode canonical decomposition, also if such a decomposition is not intended in the IPA. However, because of the nature of canonical equivalence (see Section 3.9), these two encodings are completely identical in any computational treatment, so this decomposition does not have any practical consequences.

5.9 Pitfall: Different notions of diacritics

Another pitfall relates to the question, what is a diacritic? The problem is that the meaning of the term DIACRITIC as used by the IPA is not the same as it is used in the Unicode Standard. Specifically, diacritics in the IPA-sense are either so-called COMBINING DIACRITICAL MARKS or SPACING MODIFIER LETTERS in the Unicode Standard. Crucially, Combining Diacritical Marks are by definition combined with the character before them (to form so-called default grapheme clusters, see Chapter 2). In contrast, Spacing Modifier Letters are by definition *not* combined into grapheme clusters with the preceding character, but simply treated as separate letters. In the context of the IPA, the following IPA-diacritics are actually Spacing Modifier Letters in the Unicode Standard:

Length marks, namely:

<◌ː> MODIFIER LETTER TRIANGULAR COLON at U+02D0
<◌ˑ> MODIFIER LETTER HALF TRIANGULAR COLON at U+02D1

Tone letters, including but not limited to:

<˥> MODIFIER LETTER EXTRA-HIGH TONE BAR at U+02E5
<˩> MODIFIER LETTER LOW TONE BAR at U+02E8

Superscript letters, including but not limited to:[12]

<◌ʰ> MODIFIER LETTER SMALL H at U+02B0
<◌ˤ> MODIFIER LETTER SMALL REVERSED GLOTTAL STOP at U+02E4
<◌ⁿ> SUPERSCRIPT LATIN SMALL LETTER N at U+207F

The rhotic hook:[13]

<◌˞> MODIFIER LETTER RHOTIC HOOK at U+02DE

Although linguists might expect these characters to belong together with the character in front of them, at least for tone letters, stress symbols and <ʰ> MODI-

[12] The Unicode Standard defines the *Phonetic Extensions* block that defines symbols used in phonetic notation systems, including the Uralic Phonetic Alphabet, Americanist and Russianist phonetic notations, Oxford English and American dictionaries, etc. Among other symbols, the *Phonetic Extensions* block includes the superscript letters <ᵐ, ᵑ, ᵇ>, which are not valid IPA characters, although we have seen them used in linguistic practice.

[13] It is really unfortunate that the rhotic hook in Unicode is classified as a Spacing Modifier, and not as a Combining Diacritical Mark. Although the rhotic hook is placed to the right of its base character (and not above or below), it still is always connected to the character in front, even physically connected to it. We cannot find any reason for this treatment, and consider it an error in Unicode. We hope it will be possible to change this classification in the future.

FIER LETTER SMALL H at U+02B0 the Unicode Consortium's decision to treat it as a separate character is also linguistically correct.

- According to the IPA, <ʰ> can be used both as <◌ʰ> for post-aspiration (following the base character) and as <ʰ◌> for pre-aspiration (preceding the base character), so there is no consistent direction in which this diacritic should bind. Note that there is yet another homoglyph, namely the COMBINING LATIN SMALL LETTER H at U+036A. We propose not to use this combining diacritical mark, but to standardize on Unicode modifier letters for all superscript letters in IPA.
- Tone letters <˥, ˦, ˧, ˨, ˩> from U+02E5–U+02E9 are normally written at the end of the syllable, possibly occurring immediately adjacent to a consonant in the coda of the syllable. Such tone markers should of course not be treated as belonging to this consonant, so we propose to treat tone letters as separate segments.
- Stress markers <ˈ◌> at U+02C8 and <ˌ◌> at U+02CC have a very similar distribution in that they normally are written at the start of the stressed syllable. In a sense, they thus belong to the characters following the stress marker, but it would be wrong to cluster them together with whatever segment is at the start of the syllable. So, like tone letters, we propose to treat stress markers as separate segments.

If intended, then any default combination of Spacing Modifiers with the preceding character can be specified in orthography profiles (see Chapter 7).

5.10 Pitfall: No unique diacritic ordering

Also related to diacritics is the question of ordering. To our knowledge, the International Phonetic Association does not specify an ordering for diacritics that combine with phonetic base symbols; this exercise is left to the reasoning of the transcriber. However, such marks have to be explicitly ordered if sequences of them are to be interoperable and compatible computationally. An example is a labialized aspirated alveolar plosive: <tʷʰ>. There is nothing holding linguists back from using <tʰʷ> instead (with exactly the same intended meaning). However, from a technical standpoint, these two sequences are different; if both sequences are used in a document, searching for <tʷʰ> will not find any instances of <tʰʷ>, and vice versa. Likewise, a creaky voiced syllabic dental nasal can be encoded in various orders, e.g. <n̪̰̩>, <n̩̰̪> or <n̩̪̰>.

Canonical combining classes

In accordance with the absence of any specification of ordering in the IPA, the Unicode Standard likewise does not propose any standardized orders. Both leave it to the user to be consistent; this approach naturally invites inconsistency across different authored resources.

There is one (minor) aspect of ordering for which the Unicode Standard does present a canonical solution. Fortunately, this is uncontroversial from a linguistic perspective. Diacritics in the Unicode Standard (i.e. Combining Diacritical Marks, see Section 5.9) are classified in so-called canonical combining classes. In practice, the diacritics are distinguished by their position relative to the base character.[14] When applying a Unicode normalization (NFC or NFD, see Section 3.9), the diacritics in different positions are put in a specified order. This process therefore harmonizes the difference between different encodings in some situations, for example in the case of an extra-short creaky voice vowel <ḛ̆>. This grapheme cluster can be encoded either as <e>+<◌̆>+<◌̰> or as <e>+<◌̰>+<◌̆>. To prevent this twofold encoding, the Unicode Standard specifies the second ordering as canonical (namely, diacritics below are put before diacritics above).

When encoding a string according to the Unicode Standard, it is possible to do this either using the NFC (composition) or NFD (decomposition) normalization (see Section 3.9). Decomposition implies that precomposed characters (like <á> latin small letter a with acute at U+00E1) will be split into its parts. This might sound preferable for a linguistic analysis, as the different diacritics are separated from the base characters. However, note that most attached elements like strokes (e.g. in the <ɨ>), retroflex hooks (e.g. in <ʐ>) or rhotic hooks (e.g. in <ɝ>) will not be decomposed. In general, Unicode decomposition does not behave like a feature decomposition as expected from a linguistic perspective. It is thus important to consider Unicode decomposition only as a technical procedure, and not assume that it is linguistically sensible.

Proposal for diacritic ordering

Facing the problem of specifying a consistent ordering of diacritics while developing a large database of phonological inventories from the world's languages, Moran (2012: 540) defined a set of diacritic ordering conventions. The conventions are influenced by the linguistic literature, though some ad-hoc decisions had to be taken given the vast variability of phonological segments described

[14]For a detailed description, see: http://unicode.org/reports/tr44/#Canonical_Combining_Class_Values.

by linguists. The most recent version of the conventions is published online by Moran & McCloy (2014).[15]

According to Unicode Canonical Combining Classes, overlay diacritics like <◌̴> (Combining Class number 1) always come before diacritics below (Combining Class number 220), which in turn always come before diacritics above (Combining Class number 230), which in turn come before diacritics over multiple characters like the tie bar <◌͡◌> (Combining Class number 233). We follow this order, but add the other IPA diacritics (which are not diacritics in the Unicode sense) between diacritics below and the tie bar. Further, *within* all these classes of diacritics there is no canonical ordering specified by Unicode, so we propose an explicit ordering here.

Starting with the diacritics below: if a character sequence contains more than one diacritic below the base character, then the place features are applied first (linguolabial, dental, apical, laminal, advanced, retracted), followed by the manner features (raised, lowered, advanced and retracted tongue root), then secondary articulations (more round, less round), laryngeal settings (creaky, breathy, voiced, devoiced), and finally the syllabic or non-syllabic marker. So, the order that is proposed is the following, where <|> indicates *or* and <⟶> indicates *precedes*. Note that the groups of alternatives (as marked by <|>) are supposed never to occur together with the same base character. In effect, this represents yet another restriction on possible diacritic sequences.

Combining Diacritical Marks (below) ordering:

⟶ linguolabial <◌̼> | dental <◌̪> | apical <◌̺> | laminal <◌̻>
⟶ advanced <◌̟> | retracted <◌̠>
⟶ raised <◌̝> | lowered <◌̞>
⟶ advanced tongue root <◌̘> | retracted tongue root <◌̙>
⟶ more rounded <◌̹> | less rounded <◌̜>
⟶ creaky voiced <◌̰> | breathy voiced <◌̤> | voiced <◌̬> | voiceless <◌̥>
⟶ syllabic <◌̩> | non-syllabic <◌̯>

Next, if a character sequence contains more than one diacritic above the base character, we propose the following order:

Combining Diacritical Marks (above) ordering:

⟶ nasalized <◌̃>
⟶ centralized <◌̈> | mid-centralized <◌̽>

[15] http://phoible.github.io/conventions/

→ extra short <◌̆>
→ no audible release <◌̚ >

Then, when a character sequence contains more than one character of the Spacing Modifier Letters, these will be placed after all combining diacritical marks in the following order:

Spacing Modifier Letters ordering:

→ rhotic hook <◌˞>
→ lateral release <◌ˡ> | nasal release <◌ⁿ>
→ labialized <◌ʷ>
→ palatalized <◌ʲ>
→ velarized <◌ˠ>
→ pharyngealized <◌ˤ>
→ aspirated <◌ʰ> | ejective <◌’>
→ long <◌ː> | half-long <◌ˑ>

Finally, the tie bar follows at the very end of any such sequence:

Tie bar:

→ tie bar <◌͡◌>

5.11 Pitfall: Revisions to the IPA

With each revision of the IPA, many decisions need to be made by the Association as to which symbols should be added, removed or changed. For example, in the 1989 revision of the IPA at the Kiel Convention, changes to specific symbols (in previous charts) were debated and the Association's members made certain decisions. The prevailing mood at the convention was not to change specific symbols unless a strong case was made (Ladefoged 1990). For example, two such decisions included:

- Symbols for clicks were changed from <ʇ ʖ ʗ> to <| ‖ !> because the latter were the symbols used by nearly all Khoisanists and Bantuists.
- The Americanist tradition of using using <◌̌>, a combining caron at U+030C for all postalveolar sounds, like in <š ž č ǰ>, was not adopted because the Association members at the convention "were not sufficiently impressed by arguments ... to the effect that these sounds formed a natural class, and thus is would be appropriate to recognize this by maintaining a common aspect to their symbolism" (Ladefoged 1990: 62).

These decisions have practical consequences for transcribers of IPA, particularly those who wish to follow current recommended practices of encoding electronic text in the Unicode Standard. For example, the Unicode Standard contains LATIN SMALL LETTER TURNED T <ʇ> at U+0287, which is no longer part of the IPA. It still exists, however, in the Unicode IPA EXTENSIONS block, with the comment "dental click (sound of 'tsk tsk')". In such cases, the IPA transcriber must know the status of legacy symbols in the current version of the IPA and the correct characters in the Unicode Standard.

The most controversial issue regarding symbols debated at the convention was the representation for voiceless implosives (Ladefoged 1990: 62). In accordance with the principles of the IPA, as outlined in Section 4, distinct symbols are favored for cases of phonological contrast. Further, convenience of display in the chart must also be taken into account when arguing for or against the inclusion or deletion of IPA symbols in the IPA chart. Finally, the inclusion or deletion of symbols should consider the current state of phonetic knowledge of the world's languages.

Ladefoged (1990) argued against the inclusion of the symbols < ƥ, ƭ, ƈ, ƙ, ʠ > for voiceless implosives, noting (i) that they are not contrastive (e.g. in Mayan languages); (ii) that there is no instrumental evidence supporting voiceless implosives in Africa; and (iii) that the sounds are sufficiently rare so as not to need a whole new row of symbols in the chart. Ladefoged favored symbolizing the sounds using a voiceless diacritic ring below voiced implosives, e.g. <ɓ̥>. Nevertheless, in the 1989 IPA chart there is indeed a row for implosives containing voiceless and voiced pairs.[16] But in the next revision, in 1993 (with an update in 1996), the voiceless implosives were dropped. The implosives row from the IPA consonantal chart disappeared and voiced implosives were given a column in the non-pulmonic consonants table (which is still reflected in the latest revision to date, IPA 2005).

The *Journal of the International Phonetic Association* follows its own published standard for the IPA at the time of publication, even when it may conflict with the Association's principle of using different symbols for contrastive sounds and diacritics for phonetic variation. For example, in the case of voiceless implosives, McLaughlin (2005) shows that Seereer-Siin (Niger-Congo, Atlantic; ISO 639-3 srr) has a phonologically contrastive set of voiced and voiceless implosive stops at the labial, coronal and palatal places of articulation. These symbols are transcribed in an *Illustrations of the IPA* article in the IPA journal as < ɓ̥, ɗ̥, ʄ̥ >.

[16] https://en.wikipedia.org/wiki/File:IPA_as_of_1989.png

The point of this pitfall is to highlight that revisions to the IPA will continue into the future, albeit infrequently. Nevertheless, given the Unicode Standard's principle of maintaining backwards compatibility (at all costs), transcribers and consumers of IPA cannot rely solely on remarks in the Unicode Standard to reflect current standard IPA usage. There is the possibility that at a later revision of the IPA, symbols that are not currently encoded in the Unicode Standard will be added to the IPA – although we think this is unlikely.

5.12 Additions to the IPA

In the course of collecting a large sample of phoneme systems across the world's languages, Moran et al. (2014) found that in order to preserve distinctions both within and across language descriptions, additions to the approved IPA glyph set were needed. Wherever possible these additions were drawn from the extIPA symbols for disordered speech (Duckworth et al. 1990).[17] This section describes these proposed additions to the IPA glyph set. The additions are not part of the official IPA recommendations, so they should be used with caution.

- Retroflex click
  Retroflex clicks can be represented by <‼> double exclamation mark at U+203C. Note that the (post-)alveolar click <!> at U+01C3 is confusingly referred to as latin letter retroflex click in the Unicode Standard, which is probably best considered an error.
- Voiced retroflex implosive
  Although the IPA includes a series of voiced implosives (marked with a hook on top, see Section 5.8), there is no voiced retroflex implosive. Following the spirit of the IPA, we propose to use <ᶑ> latin small letter d with hook and tail at U+1D91 for this sound.
- Fortis/lenis
  Languages described as having a fortis/plain/lenis distinction that corresponds poorly with the traditional voiced/voiceless-unaspirated/voiceless-aspirated continuum can be marked using the voiceless glyph for the plain phoneme, and then <◌͈> combining double vertical line below at U+0348 to mark the fortis articulation, and/or <◌͉> combining left angle below at U+0349 for the lenis articulation.
- Frictionalization
  The diacritic <◌͓> combining x below at U+0353 can be used to represent

[17] https://www.internationalphoneticassociation.org/sites/default/files/extIPAChart2008.pdf

three types of frictionalized sounds: First, click consonants where the release of the anterior closure involves an ingressive sucking sound similar to a fricative, for example <k!͓ʰ>; second, frictionalized vowels (sounds that are phonologically vocalic, but with sufficiently close closures to create buzzing); and third, fricative sounds at places of articulation that do not have dedicated fricative glyphs, for example sounds with voiceless velar lateral frication, like <ʟ̥͓>.

- Derhoticization
  For derhoticization we propose to use <◌̮> combining breve below at U+032E.
- Coronal non-sibilant
  Languages described as having a sibilant/non-sibilant distinction among coronal fricatives and affricates can be handled using the subscript <◌͇> combining equals sign below at U+0347 to mark the non-sibilant phoneme.
- Glottalization
  Glottalized sounds can be indicated using <◌ˀ> modifier letter glottal stop at U+02C0, unless it is clear that either ejective or creaky voicing are the intended sounds (in which cases the standard IPA diacritics should be used). Pre-glottalized sounds can be marked with <ˀ◌> to the left of the base glyph, for example <ˀt>.
- Voiced pre-aspiration
  Voiced sounds having pre-aspiration can be marked with <ʱ◌> modifier letter small h with hook at U+02B1 to the left of the base glyph, for example <ʱd>.
- Epilaryngeal phonation
  There are some rare articulations that make use of an epilaryngeal phonation mechanism (e.g. the "sphincteric vowels" of !Xóõ). To represent these vowels, we propose to use the modifier <◌ᴱ> modifier letter capital e at U+1D31 to denote such sphincteric phonation.

5.13 Unicode IPA Recommendations

Summarizing the pitfalls as discussed in this chapter, we propose to define three different IPA encodings: strict-IPA, valid-IPA and widened-IPA. Informally speaking, valid-IPA represents the current state of the IPA (The International Phonetic Association 2015). Strict-IPA represents a more constrained version of IPA, while widened-IPA is a slightly extended version of IPA, allowing a few more symbols.

Strict-IPA encoding is supposed to be used when interoperability of phonetic resources is intended. It is a strongly constrained subset of IPA geared towards uniqueness of encoding. Ideally, for each transcription there should be exactly one possible strict-IPA encoding. For each phonetic feature there is only one possibility (see Section 5.5) and the IPA diacritics are forced into a canonical ordering (see Section 5.10).

Valid-IPA does allow alternative symbols with the same phonetic meaning, as specified in the official IPA specifications. Also, valid-IPA does not enforce a specific ordering of diacritics, because the IPA does not propose any such ordering. This means that in valid-IPA the same phonetic intention can be encoded in multiple ways. This is sufficient for phonetically trained human eyes, but it is not sufficient for automatic interoperability.

Finally, widened-IPA includes a few more symbols which seem to be useful for various special cases (see Section 5.12).

At the end of this chapter we have added a few longish tables summarizing all 159 different Unicode code points that form the basis of strict-IPA encoding (107 letters, 36 diacritics and 16 remaining symbols). We also make these tables available online in CSV format.[18] Each of these tables shows a typical glyph, and then lists the Unicode Code point, Unicode Name and IPA description for each symbol. Further, there is a table with the additional options for valid-IPA and a table with the additional options for widened-IPA.

- STRICT-IPA LETTERS
  The 107 different IPA letters as allowed in strict-IPA encoding are listed in Table 5.1 starting on page 73.
- STRICT-IPA DIACRITICS
  The 36 different IPA diacritics and tone markers (both Unicode Modifier Letters and Combining Diacritical Marks) as allowed in strict-IPA encoding are listed in Table 5.2 starting on page 76.
- STRICT-IPA REMAINDERS
  The 16 remaining IPA symbols (boundary, stress, tone letters and intonation markers) as allowed in strict-IPA encoding are listed in Table 5.3 on page 77.

[18] https://github.com/unicode-cookbook/cookbook/tree/master/book/tables

- VALID-IPA ADDITIONS
  The 16 additional symbols as allowed in valid-IPA encoding are listed in Table 5.4 on page 78.
- WIDENED-IPA ADDITIONS
  The 10 proposed additions to the IPA are listed in Table 5.5 on page 79.

Table 5.1: Strict-IPA letters with Unicode encodings

	Code	Unicode name	IPA name
a	U+0061	LATIN SMALL LETTER A	open front unrounded
æ	U+00E6	LATIN SMALL LETTER AE	raised open front unrounded
ɐ	U+0250	LATIN SMALL LETTER TURNED A	lowered schwa
ɑ	U+0251	LATIN SMALL LETTER ALPHA	open back unrounded
ɒ	U+0252	LATIN SMALL LETTER TURNED ALPHA	open back rounded
b	U+0062	LATIN SMALL LETTER B	voiced bilabial plosive
ʙ	U+0299	LATIN LETTER SMALL CAPITAL B	voiced bilabial trill
ɓ	U+0253	LATIN SMALL LETTER B WITH HOOK	voiced bilabial implosive
c	U+0063	LATIN SMALL LETTER C	voiceless palatal plosive
ç	U+00E7	LATIN SMALL LETTER C WITH CEDILLA	voiceless palatal fricative
ɕ	U+0255	LATIN SMALL LETTER C WITH CURL	voiceless alveolo-palatal fricative
d	U+0064	LATIN SMALL LETTER D	voiced alveolar plosive
ð	U+00F0	LATIN SMALL LETTER ETH	voiced dental fricative
ɖ	U+0256	LATIN SMALL LETTER D WITH TAIL	voiced retroflex plosive
ɗ	U+0257	LATIN SMALL LETTER D WITH HOOK	voiced dental/alveolar implosive
e	U+0065	LATIN SMALL LETTER E	close-mid front unrounded
ə	U+0259	LATIN SMALL LETTER SCHWA	mid-central schwa
ɛ	U+025B	LATIN SMALL LETTER OPEN E	open-mid front unrounded
ɘ	U+0258	LATIN SMALL LETTER REVERSED E	close-mid central unrounded
ɜ	U+025C	LATIN SMALL LETTER REVERSED OPEN E	open-mid central unrounded
ɞ	U+025E	LATIN SMALL LETTER CLOSED REVERSED OPEN E	open-mid central rounded
f	U+0066	LATIN SMALL LETTER F	voiceless labiodental fricative
ɡ	U+0261	LATIN SMALL LETTER SCRIPT G	voiced velar plosive
ɢ	U+0262	LATIN LETTER SMALL CAPITAL G	voiced uvular plosive
ɠ	U+0260	LATIN SMALL LETTER G WITH HOOK	voiced velar implosive
ʛ	U+029B	LATIN LETTER SMALL CAPITAL G WITH HOOK	voiced uvular implosive
ɤ	U+0264	LATIN SMALL LETTER RAMS HORN	close-mid back unrounded
ɣ	U+0263	LATIN SMALL LETTER GAMMA	voiced velar fricative
h	U+0068	LATIN SMALL LETTER H	voiceless glottal fricative
ħ	U+0127	LATIN SMALL LETTER H WITH STROKE	voiceless pharyngeal fricative
ʜ	U+029C	LATIN LETTER SMALL CAPITAL H	voiceless epiglottal fricative

continued on next page

Table 5.1 Strict-IPA letters with Unicode encodings – *continued*

	Code	Unicode name	IPA name
ɦ	U+0266	LATIN SMALL LETTER H WITH HOOK	voiced glottal fricative
ɧ	U+0267	LATIN SMALL LETTER HENG WITH HOOK	simultaneous voiceless postalveolar+velar fricative
ɥ	U+0265	LATIN SMALL LETTER TURNED H	voiced labial-palatal approximant
i	U+0069	LATIN SMALL LETTER I	close front unrounded
ɪ	U+026A	LATIN LETTER SMALL CAPITAL I	lax close front unrounded
ɨ	U+0268	LATIN SMALL LETTER I WITH STROKE	close central unrounded
j	U+006A	LATIN SMALL LETTER J	voiced palatal approximant
ʝ	U+029D	LATIN SMALL LETTER J WITH CROSSED TAIL	voiced palatal fricative
ɟ	U+025F	LATIN SMALL LETTER DOTLESS J WITH STROKE	voiced palatal plosive
ʄ	U+0284	LATIN SMALL LETTER DOTLESS J WITH STROKE AND HOOK	voiced palatal implosive
k	U+006B	LATIN SMALL LETTER K	voiceless velar plosive
l	U+006C	LATIN SMALL LETTER L	voiced alveolar lateral approximant
ʟ	U+029F	LATIN LETTER SMALL CAPITAL L	voiced velar lateral approximant
ɬ	U+026C	LATIN SMALL LETTER L WITH BELT	voiceless alveolar lateral fricative
ɭ	U+026D	LATIN SMALL LETTER L WITH RETROFLEX HOOK	voiced retroflex lateral approximant
ɮ	U+026E	LATIN SMALL LETTER LEZH	voiced alveolar lateral fricative
ʎ	U+028E	LATIN SMALL LETTER TURNED Y	voiced palatal lateral approximant
m	U+006D	LATIN SMALL LETTER M	voiced bilabial nasal
ɱ	U+0271	LATIN SMALL LETTER M WITH HOOK	voiced labiodental nasal
n	U+006E	LATIN SMALL LETTER N	voiced alveolar nasal
ɴ	U+0274	LATIN LETTER SMALL CAPITAL N	voiced uvular nasal
ɲ	U+0272	LATIN SMALL LETTER N WITH LEFT HOOK	voiced palatal nasal
ɳ	U+0273	LATIN SMALL LETTER N WITH RETROFLEX HOOK	voiced retroflex nasal
ŋ	U+014B	LATIN SMALL LETTER ENG	voiced velar nasal
o	U+006F	LATIN SMALL LETTER O	close-mid back rounded
ø	U+00F8	LATIN SMALL LETTER O WITH STROKE	close-mid front rounded
œ	U+0153	LATIN SMALL LIGATURE OE	open-mid front rounded
ɶ	U+0276	LATIN LETTER SMALL CAPITAL OE	open front rounded
ɔ	U+0254	LATIN SMALL LETTER OPEN O	open-mid back rounded
ɵ	U+0275	LATIN SMALL LETTER BARRED O	close-mid central rounded

continued on next page

Table 5.1 Strict-IPA letters with Unicode encodings — *continued*

	Code	Unicode name	IPA name
p	U+0070	LATIN SMALL LETTER P	voiceless bilabial plosive
ɸ	U+0278	LATIN SMALL LETTER PHI	voiceless bilabial fricative
q	U+0071	LATIN SMALL LETTER Q	voiceless uvular plosive
r	U+0072	LATIN SMALL LETTER R	voiced alveolar trill
ʀ	U+0280	LATIN LETTER SMALL CAPITAL R	voiced uvular trill
ɹ	U+0279	LATIN SMALL LETTER TURNED R	voiced alveolar approximant
ɺ	U+027A	LATIN SMALL LETTER TURNED R WITH LONG LEG	voiced alveolar lateral flap
ɻ	U+027B	LATIN SMALL LETTER TURNED R WITH HOOK	voiced retroflex approximant
ɽ	U+027D	LATIN SMALL LETTER R WITH TAIL	voiced retroflex tap
ɾ	U+027E	LATIN SMALL LETTER R WITH FISHHOOK	voiced alveolar tap
ʁ	U+0281	LATIN LETTER SMALL CAPITAL INVERTED R	voiced uvular fricative
s	U+0073	LATIN SMALL LETTER S	voiceless alveolar fricative
ʂ	U+0282	LATIN SMALL LETTER S WITH HOOK	voiceless retroflex fricative
ʃ	U+0283	LATIN SMALL LETTER ESH	voiceless postalveolar fricative
t	U+0074	LATIN SMALL LETTER T	voiceless alveolar plosive
ʈ	U+0288	LATIN SMALL LETTER T WITH RETROFLEX HOOK	voiceless retroflex plosive
u	U+0075	LATIN SMALL LETTER U	close back rounded
ʉ	U+0289	LATIN SMALL LETTER U BAR	close central rounded
ɯ	U+026F	LATIN SMALL LETTER TURNED M	close back unrounded
ɰ	U+0270	LATIN SMALL LETTER TURNED M WITH LONG LEG	voiced velar approximant
ʊ	U+028A	LATIN SMALL LETTER UPSILON	lax close back rounded
v	U+0076	LATIN SMALL LETTER V	voiced labiodental fricative
ʋ	U+028B	LATIN SMALL LETTER V WITH HOOK	voiced labiodental approximant
ⱱ	U+2C71	LATIN SMALL LETTER V WITH RIGHT HOOK	voiced labiodental tap
ʌ	U+028C	LATIN SMALL LETTER TURNED V	open-mid back unrounded
w	U+0077	LATIN SMALL LETTER W	voiced labial-velar approximant
ʍ	U+028D	LATIN SMALL LETTER TURNED W	voiceless labial-velar fricative
x	U+0078	LATIN SMALL LETTER X	voiceless velar fricative
y	U+0079	LATIN SMALL LETTER Y	close front rounded
ʏ	U+028F	LATIN LETTER SMALL CAPITAL Y	lax close front rounded
z	U+007A	LATIN SMALL LETTER Z	voiced alveolar fricative
ʐ	U+0290	LATIN SMALL LETTER Z WITH RETROFLEX HOOK	voiced retroflex fricative

continued on next page

Table 5.1 Strict-IPA letters with Unicode encodings – *continued*

	Code	Unicode name	IPA name
ʑ	U+0291	LATIN SMALL LETTER Z WITH CURL	voiced alveolo-palatal fricative
ʒ	U+0292	LATIN SMALL LETTER EZH	voiced postalveolar fricative
ʔ	U+0294	LATIN LETTER GLOTTAL STOP	voiceless glottal plosive
ʕ	U+0295	LATIN LETTER PHARYNGEAL VOICED FRICATIVE	voiced pharyngeal fricative
ʡ	U+02A1	LATIN LETTER GLOTTAL STOP WITH STROKE	epiglottal plosive
ʢ	U+02A2	LATIN LETTER REVERSED GLOTTAL STOP WITH STROKE	voiced epiglottal fricative
ǀ	U+01C0	LATIN LETTER DENTAL CLICK	voiceless dental click
ǁ	U+01C1	LATIN LETTER LATERAL CLICK	voiceless alveolar lateral click
ǂ	U+01C2	LATIN LETTER ALVEOLAR CLICK	voiceless palatoalveolar click
ǃ	U+01C3	LATIN LETTER RETROFLEX CLICK	voiceless (post)alveolar click
ʘ	U+0298	LATIN LETTER BILABIAL CLICK	voiceless bilabial click
β	U+03B2	GREEK SMALL LETTER BETA	voiced bilabial fricative
θ	U+03B8	GREEK SMALL LETTER THETA	voiceless dental fricative
χ	U+03C7	GREEK SMALL LETTER CHI	voiceless uvular fricative

Table 5.2: Strict-IPA diacritics with Unicode encodings

	Code	Unicode name	IPA name
◌̴	U+0334	COMBINING TILDE OVERLAY	velarized or pharyngealized
◌̼	U+033C	COMBINING SEAGULL BELOW	linguolabial
◌̪	U+032A	COMBINING BRIDGE BELOW	dental
◌̻	U+033B	COMBINING SQUARE BELOW	laminal
◌̺	U+033A	COMBINING INVERTED BRIDGE BELOW	apical
◌̟	U+031F	COMBINING PLUS SIGN BELOW	advanced
◌̠	U+0320	COMBINING MINUS SIGN BELOW	retracted
◌̝	U+031D	COMBINING UP TACK BELOW	raised
◌̞	U+031E	COMBINING DOWN TACK BELOW	lowered
◌̘	U+0318	COMBINING LEFT TACK BELOW	advanced tongue root
◌̙	U+0319	COMBINING RIGHT TACK BELOW	retracted tongue root

continued on next page

Table 5.2 Strict-IPA diacritics with Unicode encodings – *continued*

	Code	Unicode name	IPA name
◌̜	U+031C	COMBINING LEFT HALF RING BELOW	less rounded
◌̹	U+0339	COMBINING RIGHT HALF RING BELOW	more rounded
◌̬	U+032C	COMBINING CARON BELOW	voiced
◌̥	U+0325	COMBINING RING BELOW	voiceless
◌̰	U+0330	COMBINING TILDE BELOW	creaky voiced
◌̤	U+0324	COMBINING DIAERESIS BELOW	breathy voiced
◌̩	U+0329	COMBINING VERTICAL LINE BELOW	syllabic
◌̯	U+032F	COMBINING INVERTED BREVE BELOW	non-syllabic
◌̃	U+0303	COMBINING TILDE	nasalized
◌̈	U+0308	COMBINING DIAERESIS	centralized
◌̽	U+033D	COMBINING X ABOVE	mid-centralized
◌̆	U+0306	COMBINING BREVE	extra-short
◌̚	U+031A	COMBINING LEFT ANGLE ABOVE	no audible release
◌˞	U+02DE	MODIFIER LETTER RHOTIC HOOK	rhotacized
◌ˡ	U+02E1	MODIFIER LETTER SMALL L	lateral release
◌ⁿ	U+207F	SUPERSCRIPT LATIN SMALL LETTER N	nasal release
◌ʷ	U+02B7	MODIFIER LETTER SMALL W	labialized
◌ʲ	U+02B2	MODIFIER LETTER SMALL J	palatalized
◌ˠ	U+02E0	MODIFIER LETTER SMALL GAMMA	velarized
◌ˤ	U+02E4	MODIFIER LETTER SMALL REVERSED GLOTTAL STOP	pharyngealized
◌ʰ	U+02B0	MODIFIER LETTER SMALL H	aspirated
◌ʼ	U+02BC	MODIFIER LETTER APOSTROPHE	ejective
◌ː	U+02D0	MODIFIER LETTER TRIANGULAR COLON	long
◌ˑ	U+02D1	MODIFIER LETTER HALF TRIANGULAR COLON	half-long
◌͡◌	U+0361	COMBINING DOUBLE INVERTED BREVE	tie bar

Table 5.3: Other Strict-IPA symbols with Unicode encodings

Code	Unicode name	IPA name

continued on next page

Table 5.3 Other Strict-IPA symbols with Unicode encodings – *continued*

	Code	Unicode name	IPA name
ˈ	U+02C8	MODIFIER LETTER VERTICAL LINE	primary stress
ˌ	U+02CC	MODIFIER LETTER LOW VERTICAL LINE	secondary stress
˥	U+02E5	MODIFIER LETTER EXTRA-HIGH TONE BAR	extra high tone
˦	U+02E6	MODIFIER LETTER HIGH TONE BAR	high tone
˧	U+02E7	MODIFIER LETTER MID TONE BAR	mid tone
˨	U+02E8	MODIFIER LETTER LOW TONE BAR	low tone
˩	U+02E9	MODIFIER LETTER EXTRA-LOW TONE BAR	extra low tone
↑	U+2191	UPWARDS ARROW	global rise
↓	U+2193	DOWNWARDS ARROW	global fall
↗	U+2197	NORTH EAST ARROW	global rise
↘	U+2198	SOUTH EAST ARROW	global fall
	U+0020	SPACE	word break
.	U+002E	FULL STOP	syllable break
		U+007C	VERTICAL LINE	minor group break (foot)
‖	U+2016	DOUBLE VERTICAL LINE	major group break (intonation)
‿	U+203F	UNDERTIE	linking (absence of a break)

Table 5.4: Additional characters for valid-IPA with Unicode encodings

	Code	Unicode name	Phonetic description
◌̊	U+030A	COMBINING RING ABOVE	voiceless (above)
g	U+0067	LATIN SMALL LETTER G	voiced velar plosive
◌̋	U+030B	COMBINING DOUBLE ACUTE ACCENT	extra high tone
◌́	U+0301	COMBINING ACUTE ACCENT	high tone
◌̄	U+0304	COMBINING MACRON	mid tone
◌̀	U+0300	COMBINING GRAVE ACCENT	low tone
◌̏	U+030F	COMBINING DOUBLE GRAVE ACCENT	extra low tone
◌̂	U+0302	COMBINING CIRCUMFLEX ACCENT	falling
◌̌	U+030C	COMBINING CARON	rising
◌᷄	U+1DC4	COMBINING MACRON-ACUTE	high rising

continued on next page

Table 5.4 Additional characters for valid-IPA with Unicode encodings – *continued*

	Code	Unicode name	Phonetic description
◌᷅	U+1DC5	COMBINING GRAVE-MACRON	low rising
◌᷆	U+1DC6	COMBINING MACRON-GRAVE	low falling
◌᷇	U+1DC7	COMBINING ACUTE-MACRON	high falling
◌᷈	U+1DC8	COMBINING GRAVE-ACUTE-GRAVE	rising-falling
◌᷉	U+1DC9	COMBINING ACUTE-GRAVE-ACUTE	falling-rising
◌͜◌	U+035C	COMBINING DOUBLE BREVE BELOW	tie bar (below)

Table 5.5: Additions to widened-IPA with Unicode encodings

	Code	Unicode name	Phonetic description
‼	U+203C	DOUBLE EXCLAMATION MARK	retroflex click
ᶑ	U+1D91	LATIN SMALL LETTER D WITH HOOK AND TAIL	voiced retroflex implosive
◌͈	U+0348	COMBINING DOUBLE VERTICAL LINE BELOW	fortis
◌͉	U+0349	COMBINING LEFT ANGLE BELOW	lenis
◌͓	U+0353	COMBINING X BELOW	frictionalized
◌̮	U+032E	COMBINING BREVE BELOW	derhoticized
◌͇	U+0347	COMBINING EQUALS SIGN BELOW	non-sibilant
◌ˀ	U+02C0	MODIFIER LETTER GLOTTAL STOP	glottalized
ʱ◌	U+02B1	MODIFIER LETTER SMALL H WITH HOOK	voiced pre-aspirated
◌ᴱ	U+1D31	MODIFIER LETTER CAPITAL E	epilaryngeal phonation

6 Practical recommendations

This chapter is meant to be a short guide for novice users who are not interested in the programmatic aspects presented in Chapters 7 & 8. Instead, we provide links to quickly find general information about the Unicode Standard and the International Phonetic Alphabet (IPA). We target ordinary working linguists who want to know how to easily insert special characters into their digital documents and applications.

6.1 Unicode

We discussed the Unicode Consortium's approach to computationally encoding writing systems in Chapter 2. The common pitfalls that we have encountered when using the Unicode Standard are discussed in detail in Chapter 3. Together these chapters provide users with an in-depth background about the hurdles they may encounter when using the Unicode Standard for encoding their data or for developing multilingual applications. For general background information about Unicode and character encodings, see these resources:

- http://www.unicode.org/standard/WhatIsUnicode.html
- https://en.wikipedia.org/wiki/Unicode
- https://www.w3.org/International/articles/definitions-characters/

For practical purposes, users need a way to insert special characters (i.e. characters that are not easily entered via their keyboards) into documents and software applications. There are a few basic approaches for inserting special characters. One way is to use software-specific functionality, when it is available. For example, Microsoft Word has an insert-special-symbol-or-character function that allows users to scroll through a table of special characters across different scripts. Special characters can be then inserted into the document by clicking on them. Another way is to install a system-wide application for special character insertion. We have long been fans of the PopChar application from Ergonis Software, which is a small program that can insert most Unicode characters (note however that the full version requires a paid subscription).[1]

There are also web-based Unicode character pickers available through the browser that allow for the creation and insertion of special characters, which can then be copied & pasted into documents or software applications. For example, try:

- https://unicode-table.com/en/
- https://r12a.github.io/pickers/

Yet another option for special character insertion includes operating system-specific shortcuts. For example on the Mac, holding down a key on the keyboard for a second, say <u>, triggers a pop up with the options <û, ü, ù, ú, ū> which can then be inserted by keying the associated number (1–5). This method is convenient for occasionally inserting type accented characters, but the full range of special characters is limited and this method is burdensome for rapidly inserting many different characters. For complete access to special characters, Mac provides a Keyboard Viewer application available in the Keyboard pane of the System Preferences.

On Windows, accented characters can be inserted by using alt-key shortcuts, i.e. holding down the alt-key and keying in a sequence of numbers (which typically reflect the Unicode character's decimal representation). For example, LATIN SMALL LETTER C WITH CEDILLA at U+00E7 with the decimal code 231 can be inserted by holding the alt-key and keying the sequence 0231. Again, this method is burdensome for rapidly inserting characters. For access to the full range of Unicode characters, the Character Map program comes preinstalled on all Microsoft operating systems.

There are also many third-party applications that provide custom keyboard layouts. These programs typically override keys or keystrokes on the user's keyboard allowing them to quickly enter special characters (once the layout of the new keyboard is mastered). They can be language-specific or devoted specifically to IPA. Two popular programs are:

- https://keyman.com/
- http://scripts.sil.org/ipa-sil_keyboard

[1] http://www.ergonis.com/products/popcharx/

6.2 IPA

In Chapter 4 we described in detail the history and principles of the International Phonetic Alphabet (IPA) and how it became encoded in the Unicode Standard. In Chapter 5 we describe the resulting pitfalls from their marriage. These two chapters provide a detailed overview of the challenges that users face when working with the two standards.

For general information about the IPA, the standard text is the *Handbook of the International Phonetic Association: A Guide to the Use of the International Phonetic Alphabet* (The International Phonetic Association 1999). The handbook describes in detail the principles and premises of the IPA, which we have summarized in Section 4.2. The handbook also provides many examples of how to use the IPA. The Association also makes available information about itself online[2] and it provides the most current IPA charts.[3] Wikipedia also has a comprehensive article about the IPA.[4]

There are several good Unicode IPA character pickers available through the browser, including:

- https://r12a.github.io/pickers/ipa/
- https://westonruter.github.io/ipa-chart/keyboard/
- http://ipa.typeit.org/

Various linguistics departments also provide information about IPA fonts, software, and inserting Unicode IPA characters. Two useful resources are:

- http://www.phon.ucl.ac.uk/resource/phonetics/
- https://www.york.ac.uk/language/current/resources/freeware/ipa-fonts-and-software/

Regarding fonts that display Unicode IPA correctly, many linguists turn to the IPA Unicode fonts developed by SIL International. The complete SIL font list is available online.[5] There is also a page that describes IPA transcription using the SIL fonts and provides an informative discussion on deciding which font to use.[6] Traditionally, IPA fonts popular with linguists were created and maintained by SIL International, so it is often the case in our experience that we encounter

[2] https://www.internationalphoneticassociation.org/
[3] https://www.internationalphoneticassociation.org/content/ipa-chart
[4] https://en.wikipedia.org/wiki/International_Phonetic_Alphabet
[5] http://scripts.sil.org/SILFontList
[6] http://scripts.sil.org/ipahome

linguistics data in legacy IPA fonts, i.e. pre-Unicode fonts such as SIL IPA93.[7] SIL International does a good job of describing how to convert from legacy IPA fonts to Unicode IPA. The most popular Unicode IPA fonts are Doulos SIL and Charis SIL:

- https://software.sil.org/doulos/
- https://software.sil.org/charis/

Lastly, here are some online resources that we find particularly useful for finding more information about individual Unicode characters and also for converting between encodings:

- http://www.fileformat.info/
- https://unicodelookup.com/
- https://r12a.github.io/scripts/featurelist/
- https://r12a.github.io/app-conversion/

6.3 For programmers and potential programmers

If you have made it this far, and you are eager to know more about the technical aspects of the Unicode Standard and how they relate to software programming, we recommend two light-hearted blog posts on the topic. The classic blog post about what programmers should know about the Unicode Standard is Joel Spolsky's *The Absolute Minimum Every Software Developer Absolutely, Positively Must Know About Unicode and Character Sets (No Excuses!).*[8] A more recent blogpost, with a bit more of the technical details, is by David C. Zentgraf and is titled, *What Every Programmer Absolutely, Positively Needs To Know About Encodings And Character Sets To Work With Text.*[9] This post is aimed at software developers and uses the PHP language for examples.

For users of Python, see the standard documentation on how to use Unicode in your programming applications.[10] For R users we recommend the STRINGI library.[11] For LaTeX users the TIPA package is useful for inserting IPA characters into your typeset documents. See these resources:

[7] http://scripts.sil.org/FontFAQ_IPA93

[8] https://www.joelonsoftware.com/2003/10/08/the-absolute-minimum-every-software-developer-absolutely-positively-must-know-about-unicode-and-character-sets-no-excuses/

[9] http://kunststube.net/encoding/

[10] https://docs.python.org/3/howto/unicode.html

[11] https://cran.r-project.org/web/packages/stringi/index.html

- http://www.tug.org/tugboat/tb17-2/tb51rei.pdf
- https://ctan.org/pkg/tipa
- http://ptmartins.info/tex/tipacheatsheet.pdf

But we find it much easier to use the Unicode-aware XeTeX typesetting system.[12] Unicode characters can be directly inserted into your TeX documents and compiled into typeset PDF with XeLaTeX.

Lastly, we leave you with some Unicode humor for making it this far:

- https://xkcd.com/380/
- https://xkcd.com/1137/
- http://www.commitstrip.com/en/2014/06/17/unicode-7-et-ses-nouveaux-emoji/
- http://www.i18nguy.com/humor/unicode-haiku.html

[12] http://xetex.sourceforge.net/

7 Orthography profiles

7.1 Characterizing writing systems

The Unicode Standard offers a very detailed technical approach for characterizing writing systems computationally. As such, it is sometimes too complex for the day-to-day practice of many linguists, as exemplified by the need to understand the common pitfalls that we discussed in Chapters 3 & 5. Therefore, in this section we propose some simple guidelines for linguists working in multilingual environments.

Our aims for adopting a Unicode-based solution are: (i) to improve the consistency of the encoding of sources, (ii) to transparently document knowledge about the writing system (including transliteration), and (iii) to do all of that in a way that is easy and quick to manage for many different sources with many different writing systems. The central concept in our proposal is the ORTHOGRAPHY PROFILE, a simple delimited text file, that characterizes and documents a writing system. We also offer basic implementations in Python and R to assist with the production of such files, and to apply orthography profiles for consistency testing, grapheme tokenization and transliteration. Not only can orthography profiles be helpful in the daily practice of linguistics, they also succinctly document the orthographic details of a specific source, and, as such, might fruitfully be published alongside sources (e.g. in digital archives). Also, in high-level linguistic analyses in which the graphemic detail is of central importance (e.g. phonotactic or comparative-historical studies), orthography profiles can transparently document the decisions that have been taken in the interpretation of the orthography in the sources used.

Given these goals, Unicode Locales (see Chapter 2) might seem like the ideal orthography profiles. However, there are various practical obstacles preventing the use of Unicode Locales in the daily linguistic practice, namely: (i) the XML structure[1] is too verbose to easily and quickly produce or correct manually, (ii) Unicode Locales are designed for a wide scope of information (like date formats or names of weekdays) most of which is not applicable for documenting writing

[1]http://unicode.org/reports/tr35/

systems, and (iii) most crucially, even if someone made the effort to produce a technically correct Unicode Locale for a specific source at hand, then it is well-nigh impossible to deploy the description. This is because a locale description has to be submitted to and accepted by the Unicode Common Locale Data Repository. The repository is (rightly so) not interested in descriptions that only apply to a limited set of sources (e.g. descriptions for only a single dictionary).

The major challenge, then, is developing an infrastructure to identify the elements that are individual graphemes in a source, specifically for the enormous variety of sources using some kind of alphabetic writing system. Authors of source documents (e.g. dictionaries, wordlists, corpora) use a variety of writing systems that range from their own idiosyncratic transcriptions to already well-established practical or longstanding orthographies. Although the IPA is one practical choice as a sound-based normalization for writing systems (which can act as an interlingual pivot to attain interoperability across writing systems), graphemes in each writing system must also be identified and standardized if interoperability across different sources is to be achieved. In most cases, this amounts to more than simply mapping a grapheme to an IPA segment because graphemes must first be identified in context (e.g. is the sequence one sound or two sounds or both?) and strings must be tokenized, which may include taking orthographic rules into account (e.g. a nasal sound may be transcribed as <n> when it appears between two vowels, but when it appears between a vowel and a consonant it becomes a nasalized vowel <Ṽ>).

In our experience, data from each source must be individually tokenized into graphemes so that its orthographic structure can be identified and its contents can be extracted. To extract data for analysis, a source-by-source approach is required before an orthography profile can be created. For example, almost every available lexicon on the world's languages is idiosyncratic in its orthography and thus requires lexicon-specific approaches to identify graphemes in the writing system and to map graphemes to phonemes, if desired.

Our key proposal for the characterization of a writing system is to use a grapheme tokenization as an inter-orthographic pivot. Basically, any source document is tokenized by graphemes, and only then a mapping to IPA (or any other orthographic transliteration) is performed. An ORTHOGRAPHY PROFILE then is a description of the units and rules that are needed to adequately model a graphemic tokenization for a language variety as described in a particular source document. An orthography profile summarizes the Unicode (tailored) graphemes and orthographic rules used to write a language (the details of the structure and assumptions of such a profile will be presented in the next section).

As an example of graphemic tokenization, note the three different levels of technical and linguistic elements that interact in the hypothetical lexical form <tsʰṍ̰shi>:

1. code points (10 text elements): t s ʰ o ◌̃ ◌̰ ◌́ s h i
2. grapheme clusters (7 text elements): t s ʰ ṍ̰ s h i
3. tailored grapheme clusters (4 text elements): tsʰ ṍ̰ sh i

In (1), the string <tsʰṍ̰shi> has been tokenized into ten Unicode code points (using NFD normalization), delimited here by space. Unicode normalization is required because sequences of code points can differ in their visual and logical orders. For example, <õ̰> is ambiguous to whether it is the sequence of <o> + <◌̃> + <◌̰> or <o> + <◌̰> + <◌̃>. Although these two variants are visually homoglyphs, computationally they are different (see Sections 5.3 & 5.4). Unicode normalization should be applied to this string to reorder the code points into a canonical order, allowing the data to be treated for search and comparison.

In (2), the Unicode code points have been logically normalized and visually organized into grapheme clusters, as specified by the Unicode Standard. The combining character sequence <õ̰> is normalized and visually grouped together. Note that the MODIFIER LETTER SMALL H at U+02B0 is not grouped with any other character. This is because it belongs to the Spacing Modifier Letters category. The Unicode Standard does not specify the direction that these characters modify a host character. For example, it can indicate either pre- or post-aspiration (whereas the nasalization or creaky diacritic is defined in the Unicode Standard to apply to a specified base character).

Finally, to arrive at the graphemic tokenization in (3), tailored grapheme clusters are needed, possibly as specified in an orthography profile. For example, an orthography profile might specify that the sequence of characters <tsʰ> form a single grapheme. The orthography profile could also specify orthographic rules, e.g. when tokenizing graphemes in English, the sequences <sh> in the forms <mishap> and <mishmash> should be treated as distinct sequences depending on their contexts.

7.2 Informal description

An orthography profile describes the Unicode code points, characters, graphemes and orthographic rules in a writing system. An orthography profile is a language-specific (and often even resource-specific) description of the units and rules that are needed to adequately model a writing system. An important assumption is that we assume a resource is encoded in Unicode or has been converted to Unicode. Any data source that the Unicode Standard is unable to capture will also not be captured by an orthography profile.

Informally, an orthography profile specifies the graphemes – in Unicode parlance TAILORED GRAPHEME CLUSTERS – that are expected to occur in any data to be analyzed or checked for consistency. These graphemes are first identified throughout the whole data, a step which we call TOKENIZATION, and simply returned as such, possibly including error messages about any parts of the data that are not specified by the orthography profile. Once the graphemes are identified, they might also be changed into other graphemes – a step which we call TRANSLITERATION. When a grapheme has different possible transliterations, then these differences should be separated by contextual specification, possibly down to listing individual exceptional cases.

The crucial difference between our current proposal and traditional computational approaches to transliteration is the strict separation between tokenization and transliteration. Most computational approaches to transliteration are based on finite-state transducers (including the transliteration as described in the Unicode Locale Data Markup Language).[2] Finite-state transducers attempt to describe the mapping from input to output string directly as a set of rewrite rules. Although such systems are computationally well understood, we feel that they are not well-suited for day-to-day linguistic practice. First, by forcing a first step of grapheme tokenization, our system tries to keep close to the logic of the writing system. Second, by separating tokenization from transliteration there is no problem with 'feeding' and 'bleeding' of rules, common with transducers (cf. Section 8.4).

Note that to deal with ambiguous parsing cases, it is still possible to use the Unicode approach of including the ZERO-WIDTH NON-JOINER character at U+200C into the text. The idea is to add this character into the text to identify cases in which a sequence of characters is *not* supposed to be a complex grapheme cluster – even though the sequence is in the orthography profile.

In practice, we foresee a workflow in which orthography profiles are iteratively refined, while at the same time inconsistencies and errors in the data to be tokenized are corrected. In some more complex use cases there might even be a need for multiple different orthography profiles to be applied in sequence (see Sections 8.3 & 8.4 on various exemplary use cases). The result of any such workflow will normally be a cleaned dataset and an explicit description of the

[2] http://www.unicode.org/reports/tr35/

orthographic structure in the form of an orthography profile. Subsequently, the orthography profiles can be easily distributed in scholarly channels alongside the cleaned data, for example in supplementary material added to journal papers or in electronic archives.

7.3 Formal specification

File Format

The formal specifications of an orthography profile (or simply PROFILE for short) are the following:

A1. A PROFILE IS A UNICODE UTF-8 ENCODED TEXT FILE that includes information pertinent to the orthography.[3]

A2. A PROFILE IS A DELIMITED TEXT FILE WITH AN OBLIGATORY HEADER LINE. A minimal profile must have a single column with the header `Grapheme`. For any additional columns, the name in the header must be specified. The actual ordering of the columns is unimportant. The header list must be delimited in the same way as the rest of the file's contents. Each record must be kept on a separate line. Separate lines with comments are not allowed. Comments that belong to specific lines must be put in a separate column of the file, e.g. add a column called COMMENTS.

A3. METADATA SHOULD BE ADDED IN A SEPARATE UTF-8 TEXT FILE using the JSON-LD dialect specified in *Metadata Vocabulary for Tabular Data*.[4] This metadata format allows for easy inclusion of Dublin Core metadata,[5] which should be used to specify information about the orthographic description in the orthography profile.[6] The orthography profile metadata should minimally include provenance information including: (i) author, (ii) date, (iii) title of the profile, and (iv) bibliographic data for resource(s) that illustrate the orthography described in the profile. Crucially, the metadata should

[3] See Section 3.12 in which we suggest to use NFC, no-BOM and LF line breaks because of the pitfalls they avoid. A keen reviewer notes, however, that specifying a convention for line endings and BOM is overly strict because most computing environments (now) transparently handle both alternatives. For example, using Python a file can be decoded using the encoding "utf-8-sig", which strips away the BOM (if present) and reads an input full in text mode, so that both line feed variants "LF" and "CRLF" will be stripped.

[4] https://www.w3.org/TR/tabular-metadata/

[5] http://dublincore.org/

[6] http://w3c.github.io/csvw/metadata/#dfn-common-property

also specify (v) a stable language identifier of the target language of the profile using BCP 47/ISO 639-3 or Glottocode as per the CLDF ontology.[7] Further, the metadata file should provide information about the orthography profile's structure and contents, including: (vi) its dialect description,[8] and (vii) proper column descriptions,[9] which describe how a column should be interpreted and processed (e.g. whether they should be processed as regular expressions; see below). Finally, in accordance with the *Metadata Vocabulary for Tabular Data*, the metadata's filename should consist of the orthography profile's filename appended with "-metadata.json".[10]

The content of a profile consists of lines, each describing a grapheme of the orthography, using the following columns:

A5. A minimal profile consists of a single column with a header called `Grapheme`, listing each of the different graphemes in a separate line. The name of this column is crucial for automatic processing.

A6. Optional columns can be used to specify the left and right context of the grapheme, to be designated with the headers `Left` and `Right` respectively. The same grapheme can occur multiple times with different contextual specifications, for example to distinguish different pronunciations depending on the context.

A7. The columns `Grapheme`, `Left` and `Right` can use regular expression metacharacters. If regular expressions are used, then they must be specified in the metadata file as such, and all literal usage of the special symbols, like full stops <.> or dollar signs <$> (so-called metacharacters) have to be explicitly escaped by adding a backslash before them (i.e. use <\.> or <\$>). Note that any specification of context automatically expects regular expressions, so it is better to always escape all regular expression metacharacters when used literally in the orthography. The following symbols will need to be preceded by a backslash: [ ] ( ) { } | + * . - ! ? ^ $ and the backslash \ itself.

A8. An optional column can be used to specify classes of graphemes, to be identified by the header `Class`. For example, this column can be used to define a class of vowels. Users can simply add ad-hoc identifiers in this

[7] http://cldf.clld.org/v1.0/terms.rdf

[8] http://w3c.github.io/csvw/metadata/#dfn-dialect-descriptions

[9] http://w3c.github.io/csvw/metadata/#dfn-datatype-description

[10] JSON-LD metadata is also the choice for datasets conforming to the Cross-Linguistic Data Formats standard, see: http://cldf.clld.org/.

column to indicate a group of graphemes, which can then be used in the description of the graphemes or the context. The identifiers should of course be chosen so that they do not conflate with any symbols used in the orthography. Note that such classes only refer to the graphemes, not to the context.

A9. Columns describing transliterations for each graphemes can be added and named at will. Often more than a single possible transliteration will be of interest. Any software application using these profiles should prompt the user to name any of these columns to select a specific transliteration.

A10. Any other columns can be added freely, but will be typically ignored by any software application using the profiles. As orthography profiles are also intended to be read and interpreted by humans, it is often very useful to add extra information about the graphemes in further columns, such as Unicode code points, Unicode names, frequency of occurrence, examples of occurrence, explanation of contextual restrictions, or comments.

Processing

For the automated processing of the profiles, the following technical standards will be expected:

B1. Each line of a profile will be interpreted according to the content type of the column as specified in the profile metadata. Content types include literal and regular expression.

B2. The class column will be used to produce explicit or chains of regular expressions, which will then be inserted in the `Grapheme`, `Left` and `Right` columns at the position indicated by the class-identifiers. For example, a class called `V` as a context specification might be replaced by a regular expression like: `(au|ei|a|e|i|o|u)`. Only the graphemes themselves are included here, not any contexts specified for the elements of the class. Note that the ordering inside this regular expression is crucial (e.g. regular expressions are greedy, so longest matches should be placed before matching substrings).

B3. The left and right contexts will be included into the regular expressions by using lookbehind and lookahead. Basically, the actual regular expression syntax of lookbehind and lookahead is simply hidden to the users by allowing them to only specify the contexts themselves. Internally, the contexts in the columns `Left` and `Right` are combined with the column `Grapheme` to form a complex regular expression like: `(?<=Left)Grapheme(?=Right)`.

B4. The regular expressions will be applied in the order as specified in the profile, from top to bottom. A software implementation can offer help in figuring out the optimal ordering of the regular expressions, but then it should be made explicit in the orthography profile because regular expressions are executed in order from top to bottom.

The actual implementation of the profile on some text-string will function as follows:

B5. All graphemes are matched in the text before they are tokenized or transliterated. In this way, there is no necessity for the user to consider *feeding* and *bleeding* situations, in which the application of a rule either changes the text so another rule suddenly applies (feeding) or prevents another rule from applying (bleeding).

B6. The matching of the graphemes can occur either globally or linearly. From a computer science perspective, the most natural way to match graphemes from a profile in some text is by walking linearly through the text-string from left to right, and at each position going through all graphemes in the profile to see which one matches, then go to the position at the end of the matched grapheme and start over. This is basically how a finite state transducer works, which is a well-established technique in computer science. However, from a linguistic point of view, our experience is that most linguists find it more natural to think from a global perspective. In this approach, the first grapheme in the profile is matched everywhere in the text-string first, before moving to the next grapheme in the profile. Theoretically, these approaches will lead to different results, though in practice of actual natural language orthographies they almost always lead to the same result. Still, we suggest that any software application using orthography profiles should offer both approaches (i.e. global or linear) to the user. The approach used should be documented in the metadata as tokenization method.

B7. The matching of the graphemes can occur either in NFC or NFD. The Unicode Standard states that software is free to compose or decompose the character stream from one representation to another. However, Unicode conformant software must treat canonically equivalent sequences in NFC and NFD as the same. It is up to the orthography profile creator how they choose to encode their profile. Several sources suggest to use NFC when possible for text encoding,[11] including SIL International with regard to data archiving.[12] In our experience, in some use cases it turns out to be practical to treat both text and profile as NFD. This typically happens when many different combinations of diacritics occur in the data. An NFD profile can then be used to first check which individual diacritics are used, before turning to the more cumbersome inspection of all combinations. We suggest that any software application using orthography profiles should offer both approaches (i.e. NFC or NFD) to the user. The approach used can be documented in the metadata as UNICODE NORMALIZATION.

B8. THE TEXT-STRING IS ALWAYS RETURNED IN TOKENIZED FORM by separating the matched graphemes by a user-specified symbols-string. Any transliteration will be returned on top of the tokenization.

B9. LEFTOVER CHARACTERS, i.e. CHARACTERS THAT ARE NOT MATCHED BY THE PROFILE, SHOULD BE REPORTED TO THE USER AS ERRORS. Typically, the unmatched characters are replaced in the tokenization by a user-specified symbol-string.

Software applications

Any software application offering to use orthography profile:

1. SHOULD OFFER USER-OPTIONS to specify:

   C1. THE NAME OF THE COLUMN TO BE USED FOR TRANSLITERATION (if any).

   C2. THE SYMBOL-STRING TO BE INSERTED BETWEEN GRAPHEMES. Optionally, a warning might be given if the chosen string includes characters from the orthography itself.

   C3. THE SYMBOL-STRING TO BE INSERTED FOR UNMATCHED STRINGS in the tokenized and transliterated output.

   C4. THE TOKENIZATION METHOD, i.e. whether the tokenization should proceed as GLOBAL or LINEAR (see B6 above).

   C5. UNICODE NORMALIZATION, i.e. whether the text-string and profile should use NFC or NFD.

2. MIGHT OFFER USER-OPTIONS:

   C6. TO ASSIST IN THE ORDERING OF THE GRAPHEMES. In our experience working with idiosyncratic transcriptions and orthographies from

[11] http://www.win.tue.nl/~aeb/linux/uc/nfc_vs_nfd.html

[12] http://scripts.sil.org/cms/scripts/page.php?item_id=NFC_vs_NFD

low-resource languages, it is helpful to identify multi-sequence graphemes before single graphemes, and to identify graphemes with context before graphemes without context. Further, frequently relevant rules might be applied after rarely relevant rules (though frequency is difficult to establish in practice, as it depends on the available data). Also, if this all fails to give any decisive ordering between rules, it seems useful to offer linguists the option to reverse the ordering from any manual specified ordering, because linguists tend to write the more general rule first, before turning to exceptions or special cases.

C7. TO ASSIST IN DEALING WITH UPPER AND LOWER CASE CHARACTERS. It seems practical to offer some basic case matching, so characters like <a> and <A> are treated equally. This will be useful in many concrete cases (such as search or collation), although the user should be warned that case matching does not function universally in the same way across orthographies.[13] Ideally, users should prepare orthography profiles with all lowercase and uppercase variants explicitly mentioned, so by default no case matching should be performed.

C8. TO TREAT THE PROFILE LITERALLY, i.e. to not interpret regular expression metacharacters. Matching graphemes literally often leads to significant speed increase, and ensures that users do not have to worry about escaping metacharacters. However, in our experience all actually interesting use cases of orthography profiles include some contexts, which automatically prevents any literal interpretation.

3. SHOULD RETURN THE FOLLOWING INFORMATION to the user:

C9. THE ORIGINAL TEXT-STRINGS to be processed in the specified Unicode normalization, i.e. in either NFC or NFD as specified by the user.

C10. THE TOKENIZED STRINGS, with additionally any transliterated strings, if transliteration is requested.

C11. A SURVEY OF ALL ERRORS ENCOUNTERED, ideally both (i) in which text-strings any errors occurred and (ii) which characters in the text-strings lead to errors.

C12. A REORDERED PROFILE, when any automatic reordering is offered.

[13] For example compare the different first-letter capitalization practices of the digraphs <Nj> and <IJ> (single-character ligatures in the Unicode Standard) in the Latin-based scripts of Southern-Slavic languages and Dutch, respectively.

8 Implementation

8.1 Overview

To illustrate the practical applications of orthography profiles, we have implemented two versions of the specifications presented in Chapter 7: one in Python[1] and one in R.[2] In this chapter, we introduce these two software libraries and provide practical step-by-step guidelines for installing and using them. Various simple and sometimes somewhat abstract examples will be discussed to show the different options available, and to illustrate the intended usage of orthography profiles in general.

Note that our two libraries have rather different implementation histories, thus they may not give the same results in all situations (as discussed in Chapter 7). However, we do provide extensive test suites for each implementation that follow standard practices to make sure that results are correct. Users should refer to these tests and to the documentation in each release for specifics about each implementation. Note that due to the different naming convention practices in Python and R, function names differ between the two libraries. Also, the performance with larger datasets may not be comparable between the Python and R implementations. In sum, our two libraries should be considered as proofs of concept and not as the final word on the practical application of the specifications discussed in the previous chapter. In our experience, the current versions are sufficiently fast and stable to be useful for academic practice (e.g. checking data consistency, or analyzing and transliterating small to medium sized data sets), but they should probably not be used for full-scale industry applications without adaptation.

First, in Section 8.2 we explain how to install Python[3] and R.[4] Then in Sections 8.3 & 8.4, we discuss our Python and R software packages, respectively. In addition to the material presented here to get users started, we maintain several case

[1]https://pypi.python.org/pypi/segments
[2]https://github.com/cysouw/qlcData
[3]https://www.python.org/
[4]https://www.r-project.org/

studies online that illustrate how to use orthography profiles in action. For convenience, we make these recipes available as Jupyter Notebooks[5] in our GitHub repository.[6] In the final section in this chapter, we also briefly describe a few recipes that we do not go into detail in this book.

8.2 How to install Python and R

When one encounters problems installing software, or bugs in programming code, search engines are your friend! Installation problems and incomprehensible error messages have typically been encountered and solved by other users. Try simply copying and pasting the output of an error message into a search engine; the solution is often already somewhere online. We are fans of Stack Exchange[7] – a network of question-and-answer websites – which are extremely helpful in solving issues regarding software installation, bugs in code, etc.

Searching the web for "install r and python" returns numerous tutorials on how to set up your machine for scientific data analysis. Note that there is no single correct setup for a particular computer or operating system. Both Python and R are available for Windows, Mac, and Unix operating systems from the Python and R project websites. Another option is to use a so-called package manager, i.e. a software program that allows the user to manage software packages and their dependencies. On Mac, we use Homebrew,[8] a simple-to-install (via the Terminal App) free and open source package management system. Follow the instructions on the Homebrew website and then use Homebrew to install R and Python (as well as other software packages such as Git and Jupyter Notebooks).

Alternatively for R, RStudio[9] provides a free and open source integrated development environment (IDE). This application can be downloaded and installed (for Mac, Windows and Unix) and it includes its own R installation and R libraries package manager. For developing in Python, we recommend the free community version of PyCharm,[10] an IDE which is available for Mac, Windows, and Unix.

Once you have R or Python (or both) installed on your computer, you are ready to use the orthography profiles software libraries presented in the next two sections. As noted above, we make this material available online on GitHub,[11] a

[5] http://jupyter.org/
[6] https://github.com/unicode-cookbook/
[7] https://stackexchange.com/
[8] https://brew.sh/
[9] https://www.rstudio.com/
[10] https://www.jetbrains.com/pycharm/
[11] https://github.com/

web-based version control system for source code management. GitHub repositories can be cloned or downloaded,[12] so that you can work through the examples on your local machine. Use your favorite search engine to figure out how to install Git on your computer and learn more about using Git.[13] In our GitHub repository, we make the material presented below (and more use cases described briefly in Section 8.5) available as Jupyter Notebooks. Jupyter Notebooks provide an interface where you can run and develop source code using the browser as an interface. These notebooks are easily viewed in our GitHub repository of use cases.[14]

8.3 Python package: segments

The Python package `segments` is available both as a command line interface (CLI) and as an application programming interface (API).

Installation

To install the Python package `segments` (Forkel & Moran 2018) from the Python Package Index (PyPI) run:

```
$ pip install segments
```

on the command line. This will give you access to both the CLI and programmatic functionality in Python scripts, when you import the `segments` library.

You can also install the `segments` package from the GitHub repository,[15] in particular if you would like to contribute to the code base:[16]

```
$ git clone https://github.com/cldf/segments
$ cd segments
$ python setup.py develop
```

Application programming interface

The `segments` API can be accessed by importing the package into Python. Here is an example of how to import the library, create a tokenizer object, tokenize a

[12] https://help.github.com/articles/cloning-a-repository/
[13] https://git-scm.com/
[14] https://github.com/unicode-cookbook/recipes
[15] https://github.com/cldf/segments
[16] https://github.com/cldf/segments/blob/master/CONTRIBUTING.md

string, and create an orthography profile. Begin by importing the `Tokenizer` from the `segments` library.

```
>>> from segments.tokenizer import Tokenizer
```

Next, instantiate a tokenizer object, which takes optional arguments for an orthography profile and an orthography profile rules file.

```
>>> t = Tokenizer()
```

The default tokenization strategy is to segment some input text at the Unicode Extended Grapheme Cluster boundaries,[17] and to return, by default, a space-delimited string of graphemes. White space between input string sequences is by default separated by a hash symbol <#>, which is a linguistic convention used to denote word boundaries. The default grapheme tokenization is useful when you encounter a text that you want to tokenize to identify potential orthographic or transcription elements.

```
>>> result = t('ĉháɾă̌ctʼɛ↗ʐː| k͡p')
>>> print(result)
>>> 'ĉ h á ɾ ă̌ c t ʼ ɛ ↗ ʐ ː | # k͡ p'

>>> result = t('ĉháɾă̌ctʼɛ↗ʐː| k͡p', segment_separator='-')
>>> print(result)
>>> 'ĉ-h-á-ɾ-ă̌-c-t-ʼ-ɛ-↗-ʐ-ː-| # k͡-p'

>>> result = t('ĉháɾă̌ctʼɛ↗ʐː| k͡p', separator=' // '))
>>> print(result)
>>> 'ĉ h á ɾ ă̌ c t ʼ ɛ ↗ ʐ ː | // k͡ p'
```

The optional `ipa` parameter forces grapheme segmentation for IPA strings.[18] Note here that Unicode Spacing Modifier Letters,[19] such as <ː> and <◌͡◌>, will be segmented together with base characters (although you might need orthography profiles and rules to correct these in your input source; see Section 5.9 for details).

```
>>> result = t('ĉháɾă̌ctʼɛ↗ʐː| k͡p', ipa=True)
>>> print(result)
>>> 'ĉ h á ɾ ă̌ c t ʼ ɛ ↗ ʐː | # k͡p'
```

[17] http://www.unicode.org/reports/tr18/tr18-19.html#Default_Grapheme_Clusters
[18] https://en.wikipedia.org/wiki/International_Phonetic_Alphabet
[19] https://en.wikipedia.org/wiki/Spacing_Modifier_Letters

You can also load an orthography profile and tokenize input strings with it. In the data directory,[20] we've placed an example orthography profile. Let's have a look at it using `more` on the command line.

```
$ more data/orthography profile.tsv
Grapheme    IPA    XSAMPA   COMMENT
a           a      a
aa          a:     a:
b           b      b
c           c      c
ch          tʃ     tS
-           NULL   NULL     "comment with    tab"
on          õ      o~
n           n      n
ih          í      i_H
inh         ĩ́      i~_H
```

An orthography profile is a delimited UTF-8 text file (here we use tab as a delimiter for reading ease). The first column must be labeled `Grapheme`, as discussed in Section 7.3. Each row in the `Grapheme` column specifies graphemes that may be found in the orthography of the input text. In this example, we provide additional columns `IPA` and `XSAMPA`, which are mappings from our graphemes to their IPA and X-SAMPA transliterations. The final column `COMMENT` is for comments; if you want to use a tab "quote that string"!

Let's load the orthography profile with our tokenizer.

```
>>> from segments.tokenizer import Profile
>>> t = Tokenizer('data/orthography profile.tsv')
```

Now let's segment the graphemes in some input strings with our orthography profile. The output is segmented given the definition of graphemes in our orthography profile, e.g. we specified the sequence of two <a a> should be a single unit <aa>, and so should the sequences <c h>, <o n> and <i h>.

```
>>> t('aabchonn-ih')
>>> 'aa b ch on n - ih'
```

This example shows how we can tokenize input text into our orthographic specification. We can also segment graphemes and transliterate them into other forms, which is useful when you have sources with different orthographies, but you

[20] https://github.com/unicode-cookbook/recipes/tree/master/Basics/data

want to be able to compare them using a single representation like IPA or X-SAMPA.

```
>>> t('aabchonn-ih', column='IPA')
>>> 'aː b tʃ õ n í'

>>> t('aabchonn-ih', column='XSAMPA')
>>> 'a: b tS o~ n i_H'
```

It is also useful to know which characters in your input string are not in your orthography profile. By default, missing characters are displayed with the Unicode REPLACEMENT CHARACTER at U+FFFD, which appears below as a white question mark within a black diamond.

```
>>> t('aa b ch on n - ih x y z')
>>> 'aa b ch on n - ih � � �'
```

You can change the default by specifying a different replacement character when you load the orthography profile with the tokenizer.

```
>>> t = Tokenizer('data/orthography-profile.tsv',
        errors_replace=lambda c: '?')
>>> t('aa b ch on n - ih x y z')
>>> 'aa b ch on n - ih ? ? ?'

>>> t = Tokenizer('data/orthography-profile.tsv',
        errors_replace=lambda c: '<{0}>'.format(c))
>>> t('aa b ch on n - ih x y z')
>>> 'aa b ch on n - ih <x> <y> <z>'
```

Perhaps you want to create an initial orthography profile that also contains those graphemes <x>, <y>, and <z>? Note that the space character and its frequency are also captured in this initial profile.

```
>>> profile = Profile.from_text('aa b ch on n - ih x y z')
>>> print(profile)

  Grapheme   frequency   mapping
             9
  a          2           a
  h          2           h
  n          2           n
  b          1           b
```

```
c           1          c
o           1          o
-           1          -
i           1          i
x           1          x
y           1          y
z           1          z
```

Command line interface

From the command line, access `segments` and its various arguments. For help, run:

```
$ segments -h
```

```
usage: segments [-h] [--verbosity VERBOSITY]
                    [--encoding ENCODING]
                    [--profile PROFILE]
                    [--mapping MAPPING]
                    command ...

Main command line interface of the segments package.

positional arguments:
  command                tokenize | profile
  args

optional arguments:
  -h, --help             show this help message and exit
  --verbosity VERBOSITY
                         increase output verbosity
  --encoding ENCODING    input encoding
  --profile PROFILE      path to an orthography profile
  --mapping MAPPING      column name in ortho profile to map
                         graphemes

Use 'segments help <cmd>' to get help about individual commands.
```

We have created some test data[21] with the German word *Schächtelchen*, which is the diminutive form of *Schachtel*, meaning ‘box’, ‘packet’, or ‘carton’ in English.

```
$ more sources/german.txt
```

```
Schächtelchen
```

We can create an initial orthography profile of the German text by passing it to the `segments profile` command. The initial profile tokenizes the text on Unicode grapheme clusters, lists the frequency of each grapheme, and provides an initial mapping column by default.

```
$ cat sources/german.txt | segments profile
```

```
Grapheme  frequency  mapping
c         3          c
h         3          h
e         2          e
S         1          S
ä         1          ä
t         1          t
l         1          l
n         1          n
```

Next, we know a bit about German orthography and which characters combine to form German graphemes. We can use the information from our initial orthography profile to hand-curate a more precise German orthography profile that takes into account capitalization (German orthography obligatorily capitalizes nouns) and grapheme clusters, such as <sch> and <ch>. We can use the initial orthography profile above as a starting point (note that, in large texts, the frequency column may signal errors in the input, such as typos, if a grapheme occurs with very low frequency). The initial orthography profile can be edited with a text editor or spreadsheet program. As per the orthography profile specifications (see Chapter 7), we can adjust rows in the `Grapheme` column and then add additional columns for transliterations or comments.

```
$ more data/german orthography profile.tsv
```

```
Grapheme  IPA  XSAMPA  COMMENT
Sch       ʃ    S       German nouns are capitalized
```

[21] https://github.com/unicode-cookbook/recipes/tree/master/Basics/sources

```
ä          ɛː   E:
ch         ç    C
t          t    t
e          e    e
l          l    l
n          n    n
```

Using the command line `segments` function and passing it our orthography profile, we can now segment our German text example into graphemes.

```
$ cat sources/german.txt | segments
  --profile=data/german-orthography-profile.tsv tokenize

'Sch ä ch t e l ch e n'
```

By providing `segments` a column for transliteration, we can convert the text into IPA.

```
$ cat sources/german.txt | segments --mapping=IPA
      --profile=data/german-orthography-profile.tsv tokenize

'ʃ ɛː ç t e l ç e n'
```

And we can transliterate to X-SAMPA.

```
$ cat sources/german.txt | segments --mapping=XSAMPA
      --profile=data/german-orthography-profile.tsv tokenize

'S E: C t e l C e n'
```

More examples are available online.[22]

8.4 R library: qlcData

Installation

The R implementation is available in the package `qlcData` (Cysouw 2018), which is directly available from the central R repository CRAN (Comprehensive R Archive Network). The R software environment itself has to be downloaded from its website.[23] After starting the included R program, the `qlcData` package for dealing with orthography profiles can be simply installed as follows:

[22] https://github.com/unicode-cookbook/recipes

[23] https://www.r-project.org

```
# download and install the qlcData software
install.packages("qlcData")
# load the software, so it can be used
library(qlcData)
```

The version available through CRAN is the latest stable version. To obtain the most recent bug-fixes and experimental additions, please use the development version, which is available on GitHub.[24] This development version can be easily installed using the github-install helper software from the `devtools` package.

```
# download and install helper software
install.packages("devtools")
# install the qlcData package from GitHub
devtools::install_github("cysouw/qlcData", build_vignettes = TRUE)
# load the software, so it can be used
library(qlcData)
```

Inside the `qlcData` package, there are two functions for orthography processing, `write.profile` and `tokenize`. The package includes help files with illustrative examples, and also a so-called vignette with explanations and examples.

```
# view help files
help(write.profile)
help(tokenize)
# view vignette with explanation and examples
vignette("orthography_processing")
```

Basically, the idea is to use `write.profile` to produce a basic orthography profile from some data and then `tokenize` to apply the (possibly edited) profile on some data, as exemplified in the next section. This can of course be performed though R, but additionally there are two more interfaces to the R code supplied in the `qlcData` package: (i) `Bash` executables and (ii) `Shiny` webapps.

The Bash executables are little files providing an interface to the R code that can be used in a shell on a UNIX-like machine. The exact location of these executables is best found after installation of R the packages. The location can be found by the following command in R.

```
# show the path to the bash executables
file.path(find.package("qlcData"), "exec")
```

These executables can be used in the resulting file path, or they can be linked and/or copied to any location as wanted. For example, a good way to use the executables in a terminal is to make softlinks (using `ln`) from the executables to a

[24] http://github.com/cysouw/qlcData

directory in your PATH, e.g. to `/usr/local/bin/`. The two executables are named `tokenize` and `writeprofile`, and the links can be made directly by using Rscript to get the paths to the executables within the terminal.

```
# get the paths to the R executables in bash
  pathT=`Rscript -e 'cat(file.path(find.package("qlcData"),
    "exec", "tokenize"))'`
  pathW=`Rscript -e 'cat(file.path(find.package("qlcData"),
    "exec", "writeprofile"))'`

  # make softlinks to the R executables in /usr/local/bin
  # you will have to enter your user's password!
  sudo ln -is $pathT $pathW /usr/local/bin
```

After inserting this softlink it should be possible to access the `tokenize` function from the shell. Try `tokenize --help` to test the functionality.

To make the functionality even more accessible, we have prepared webapps with the `Shiny` framework for the R functions. The webapps are included inside the `qlcData` package and can be started with the helper function (in R): `launch_-shiny('tokenize')`.

Profiles and error reporting

The first example of how to use these functions concerns finding errors in the encoding of texts. In the following example, it looks as if we have two identical strings, AABB. However, this is just a surface-impression delivered by the current font, which renders Latin and Cyrillic capitals identically. We can identify this problem when we produce an orthography profile from the strings. Using the R implementation of orthography profiles, we first assign the two strings to a variable `test`, and then produce an orthography profile with the function `write.profile`. As it turns out, some of the letters are Cyrillic.

```
(test <- c("AABB", "AABB"))

## [1] "AABB" "AABB"

write.profile(test)

##   Grapheme Frequency Codepoint                UnicodeName
## 1        A         3    U+0041     LATIN CAPITAL LETTER A
## 2        B         3    U+0042     LATIN CAPITAL LETTER B
## 3        A         1    U+0410  CYRILLIC CAPITAL LETTER A
## 4        B         1    U+0412 CYRILLIC CAPITAL LETTER VE
```

The function of error-message reporting can also nicely be illustrated with this example. Suppose we made an orthography profile with just the two Latin letters <A> and <B> as possible graphemes, then this profile would not be sufficient to tokenize the strings. There are graphemes in the data that are not in the profile, so the tokenization produces an error, which can be used to fix the encoding (or the profile). In the example below, we can see that the Cyrillic encoding is found in the second string of the `test` input.

```
test <- c("AABB", "АВВВ")
tokenize(test, profile = c("A", "B"))
```

```
## Warning in tokenize(test, profile = c("A", "B")):
   ## There were unknown characters found in the input data.
   ## Check output$errors for a table with all problematic strings.
```

```
## $strings
##   originals tokenized
## 1      AABB   A A B B
## 2      AABB   A ⁇ B ⁇
##
## $profile
##   Grapheme Frequency
## 1        B         3
## 2        A         3
##
## $errors
##   originals  errors
## 2      AABB A ⁇ B ⁇
##
## $missing
##   Grapheme Frequency Codepoint                UnicodeName
## 1        A         1    U+0410   CYRILLIC CAPITAL LETTER A
## 2        B         1    U+0412 CYRILLIC CAPITAL LETTER VE
```

Different ways to write a profile

The function `write.profile` can be used to prepare a skeleton for an orthography profile from some data. The preparation of an orthography profile from some data might sound like a trivial problem, but actually there are various different ways in which strings can be separated into graphemes by `write.profile`. Consider the following string of characters called `example` below. The default settings of `write.profile` separates the string into Unicode graphemes according to grapheme clusters (called user-perceived characters; see Chapter 2 for an explanation).

The results are shown in Table 8.1. As it turns out, some of these graphemes are single code points, others are combinations of two code points (see Section 3.2).

```
example <- "ÙÚÛÙÚÛ"
profile_1 <- write.profile(example)
```

Table 8.1: Profile 1 (default settings, splitting grapheme clusters)

Gr.	Freq.	Codepoint	Unicode Name
Ú	1	U+00DA	LATIN CAPITAL LETTER U WITH ACUTE
Ú	1	U+0055, U+0301	LATIN CAPITAL LETTER U, COMBINING ACUTE ACCENT
Ù	1	U+00D9	LATIN CAPITAL LETTER U WITH GRAVE
Ù	1	U+0055, U+0300	LATIN CAPITAL LETTER U, COMBINING GRAVE ACCENT
Û	1	U+00DB	LATIN CAPITAL LETTER U WITH CIRCUMFLEX
Û	1	U+0055, U+0302	LATIN CAPITAL LETTER U, COMBINING CIRCUMFLEX ACCENT

By specifying the splitting separator as the empty string `sep = ""`, it is possible to split the string into Unicode code points, thus separating the combining diacritics. The idea behind this option `sep` is that separating by a character allows for user-determined separation. The most extreme choice here is the empty string `sep = ""`, which is interpreted as separation everywhere. The other extreme is the default setting `sep = NULL`, which means that the separation is not user-defined, but relegated to the Unicode grapheme definitions. The result is shown in Table 8.2.

```
profile_2 <- write.profile(example, sep = "")
```

Table 8.2: Profile 2 (splitting by code points)

Grapheme	Frequency	Codepoint	Unicode Name
́	1	U+0301	COMBINING ACUTE ACCENT
̀	1	U+0300	COMBINING GRAVE ACCENT
̂	1	U+0302	COMBINING CIRCUMFLEX ACCENT
U	3	U+0055	LATIN CAPITAL LETTER U
Ú	1	U+00DA	LATIN CAPITAL LETTER U WITH ACUTE
Ù	1	U+00D9	LATIN CAPITAL LETTER U WITH GRAVE
Û	1	U+00DB	LATIN CAPITAL LETTER U WITH CIRCUMFLEX

Some characters look identical, although they are encoded differently. Unicode offers different ways of normalization (see Section 3.9), which can be invoked here as well using the option `normalize`. NFC normalization turns everything into the precomposed characters, while NFD normalization separates everything into base characters with combining diacritics. Splitting by code points (i.e. `sep = ""`) shows the results of these two normalizations in Tables 8.3 & 8.4.

```
# after NFC normalization Unicode code points have changed
profile_3 <- write.profile(example, normalize = "NFC", sep = "")
# NFD normalization gives another structure of the code points
profile_4 <- write.profile(example, normalize = "NFD", sep = "")
```

Table 8.3: Profile 3 (splitting by NFC code points)

Grapheme	Frequency	Codepoint	Unicode Name
Ú	2	U+00DA	LATIN CAPITAL LETTER U WITH ACUTE
Ù	2	U+00D9	LATIN CAPITAL LETTER U WITH GRAVE
Û	2	U+00DB	LATIN CAPITAL LETTER U WITH CIRCUMFLEX

Table 8.4: Profile 4 (splitting by NFD code points)

Grapheme	Frequency	Codepoint	Unicode Name
́	2	U+0301	COMBINING ACUTE ACCENT
̀	2	U+0300	COMBINING GRAVE ACCENT
̂	2	U+0302	COMBINING CIRCUMFLEX ACCENT
U	6	U+0055	LATIN CAPITAL LETTER U

It is important to realize that for Unicode grapheme definitions, NFC and NFD normalization are equivalent. This can be shown by normalizing the example in either NFD or NFC, as shown in Tables 8.5 & 8.6, by using the default separation in `write.profile`. To be precise, default separation means setting `sep = NULL`, but that has not be added explicitly below.

```
# note that NFC and NFD normalization are identical
# for Unicode grapheme definitions
profile_5 <- write.profile(example, normalize = "NFD")
profile_6 <- write.profile(example, normalize = "NFC")
```

Table 8.5: Profile 5 (splitting by graphemes after NFD)

Gr.	Freq.	Codepoint	Unicode Name
Ú	2	U+0055, U+0301	LATIN CAPITAL LETTER U, COMBINING ACUTE ACCENT
Ù	2	U+0055, U+0300	LATIN CAPITAL LETTER U, COMBINING GRAVE ACCENT
Û	2	U+0055, U+0302	LATIN CAPITAL LETTER U, COMBINING CIRCUMFLEX ACCENT

Table 8.6: Profile 6 (splitting by graphemes after NFC)

Gr.	Freq.	Codepoint	Unicode Name
Ú	2	U+00DA	LATIN CAPITAL LETTER U WITH ACUTE
Ù	2	U+00D9	LATIN CAPITAL LETTER U WITH GRAVE
Û	2	U+00DB	LATIN CAPITAL LETTER U WITH CIRCUMFLEX

These different profiles can also be produced using the bash executable `writeprofile` (see above for how to install the Bash executable). This example is also included in the help file of the executable.

Using an orthography profile skeleton

A common workflow to use these functions is to first make a skeleton for an orthography profile and then edit this profile by hand. For example, Table 8.7 shows the profile skeleton after a few graphemes have been added to the file. Note that in this example, the profile is written to the desktop, and this file has to be edited manually. We simply add a few multigraphs to the column `Grapheme` and leave the other columns empty. These new graphemes are then included in the graphemic parsing.

```
# a few words to be graphemically parsed
example <- c("mishmash", "mishap", "mischief", "scheme")
# write a profile skeleton to a file
write.profile(example, file = "~/Desktop/profile_skeleton.txt")
# edit the profile, and then use the edited profile to tokenize
tokenize(example, profile = "~/Desktop/profile_skeleton.txt")$strings
```

```
##   originals    tokenized
## 1   shampoo  sh a m p oo
## 2    mishap    m i sh a p
## 3  mischief m i sch ie f
## 4    scheme    sch e m e
```

To leave out the Unicode information in the profile skeleton, use the option `info = FALSE`. It is also possible not to use a separate file at all, but process everything within R. In simple situations this is often useful (see below), but in general we prefer to handle everything through a separately saved orthography profile. This profile often contains highly useful information that is nicely coded and saved inside this one file, and can thus be easily distributed and shared. Doing the same as above completely within R might look as follows:

Table 8.7: Manually edited profile skeleton

Grapheme	Frequency	Codepoint	UnicodeName
sh			
ch			
sch			
ie			
oo			
a	2	U+0061	LATIN SMALL LETTER A
c	2	U+0063	LATIN SMALL LETTER C
e	3	U+0065	LATIN SMALL LETTER E
f	1	U+0066	LATIN SMALL LETTER F
h	4	U+0068	LATIN SMALL LETTER H
i	3	U+0069	LATIN SMALL LETTER I
m	4	U+006D	LATIN SMALL LETTER M
o	2	U+006F	LATIN SMALL LETTER O
p	2	U+0070	LATIN SMALL LETTER P
s	4	U+0073	LATIN SMALL LETTER S

```
# make a profile, just select the column 'Grapheme'
profile <- write.profile(example)[, "Grapheme"]
# extend the profile with multigraphs
profile <- c("sh", "ch", "sch", "ie", "oo", profile)
# use the profile to tokenize
tokenize(example, profile)$strings
```

```
##   originals    tokenized
## 1   shampoo  sh a m p oo
## 2    mishap    m i sh a p
## 3  mischief m i sch ie f
## 4    scheme     sch e m e
```

Rule ordering

Everything is not yet correct with the graphemic parsing of the example discussed previously. The sequence <sh> in 'mishap' should not be a digraph, and conversely the sequence <sch> in 'mischief' should of course be separated into <s> and <ch>. One of the important issues to get the graphemic parsing right is the order in which graphemes are parsed. For example, currently the grapheme <sch> is parsed before the grapheme <ch>, leading to <m i sch ie f> instead of the intended <m i s ch ie f>. The reason that <sch> is parsed before <ch> is that by default longer graphemes are parsed before shorter ones. Our experience is that in most cases this is expected behavior. You can change the ordering by specifying the option `ordering`. Setting this option to `NULL` results in no preferential ordering, i.e. the graphemes are parsed in the order of the profile, from top to bottom. Now 'mischief' is parsed correctly, but 'scheme' is wrong. So this ordering is not the solution in this case.

```
# do not reorder the profile
# just apply the graphemes from top to bottom
tokenize( example
        , profile = "~/Desktop/profile_skeleton.txt"
        , ordering = NULL
        )$strings
```

```
##   originals      tokenized
## 1   shampoo   sh a m p oo
## 2    mishap     m i sh a p
## 3  mischief m i s ch ie f
## 4    scheme     s ch e m e
```

There are various additional options for rule ordering implemented. Please check the help description in R, i.e. `help(tokenize)`, for more details on the possible rule ordering specifications. In summary, there are four different ordering options, that can also be combined:

- SIZE
  This option orders the lines in the profile by the size of the grapheme, largest first. Size is measured by number of Unicode characters after normalization as specified in the option `normalize`. For example, <é> has a size of 1 with `normalize = "NFC"`, but a size of 2 with `normalize = "NFD"`.
- CONTEXT
  This option orders the lines by whether they have any context specified (see next section). Lines with context will then be used first. Note that this only works when the option `regex = TRUE` is also chosen (otherwise context specifications are not used).
- REVERSE
  This option orders the lines from bottom to top. Reversing order can be useful because hand-written profiles tend to put general rules before specific rules, which mostly should be applied in reverse order.
- FREQUENCY
  This option orders the lines by the frequency with which they match in the specified strings before tokenization, least frequent coming first. This frequency of course depends crucially on the available strings, so it will lead to different orderings when applied to different data. Also note that this frequency is (necessarily) measured before graphemes are identified,

so these ordering frequencies are not the same as the final frequencies shown in the output. Frequency of course also strongly differs on whether context is used for the matching through `regex = TRUE`.

By specifying more than one ordering, these orderings are used to break ties, e.g. the default setting `ordering = c("size", "context", "reverse")` will first order by size, and for those with the same size, it will order by whether there is any context specified or not. For lines that are still tied (i.e. have the same size and both/neither have context) the order will be reversed compared to the order as attested in the profile, because most hand-written specifications of graphemes will first write the general rule, followed by more specific regularities. To get the right tokenization, these rules should in most cases be applied in reverse order.

Note that different ordering of the rules does not result in feeding and bleeding effects found with finite-state rewrite rules.[25] The graphemic parsing advocated here is crucially different from rewrite rules in that there is nothing being rewritten: each line in an orthography profile specifies a grapheme to be captured in the string. All lines in the profile are processed in a specified order (as determined by the option `ordering`). At the processing of a specific line, all matching graphemes in the data are marked as captured, but not changed. Captured parts cannot be captured again, but they can still be used to match contexts of other lines in the profile. Only when all lines are processed the captured graphemes are separated (and possibly transliterated). In this way the result of the applied rules is rather easy to predict.

To document a specific case of graphemic parsing, it is highly useful to save all results of the tokenization to file by using the option `file.out`, for example as follows:

```
# save the results to various files
tokenize( example
        , profile = "~/Desktop/profile_skeleton.txt"
        , file.out = "~/Desktop/result"
        )
```

This will lead to the following four files being written. Crucially, a new profile is produced with the re-ordered orthography profile. To reproduce the tokenization, this re-ordered profile can be used with the option `ordering = NULL`.

[25] Bleeding is the effect that the application of a rule changes the string, so as to prevent a following rule from applying. Feeding is the opposite: a specific rule will only be applied because a previous rule changed the string already. The interaction of rules with such feeding and bleeding effects is extremely difficult to predict.

- RESULT_STRINGS.TSV:
  A tab-separated file with the original and the tokenized/transliterated strings.
- RESULT_PROFILE.TSV:
  A tab-separated file with the graphemes with added frequencies of occurrence in the data. The lines in the file are re-ordered according to the order that resulted from the ordering specifications (see Section 8.4).
- RESULT_ERRORS.TSV:
  A tab-separated file with all original strings that contain unmatched parts. Unmatched parts are indicated with the character as specified with the option `missing`. By default the character DOUBLE QUESTION MARK <⁇> at U+2047 is used. When there are no errors, this file is absent.
- RESULT_MISSING.TSV:
  A tab-separated file with the graphemes that are missing from the original orthography profile, as indicated in the errors. When there are no errors, then this file is absent.

Contextually specified graphemes

To refine a profile, it is also possible to add graphemes with contextual specifications. An orthography profile can have columns called `Left` and `Right` to specify the context in which the grapheme is to be separated.[26] For example, we are adding an extra line to the profile from above, resulting in the profile shown in Table 8.8. The extra line specifies that <s> is a grapheme when it occurs after <mi>. Such contextually-specified graphemes are based on regular expressions so you can also use regular expressions in the description of the context. For such contextually specified graphemes to be included in the graphemic parsing we have to specify the option `regex = TRUE`. This contextually specified grapheme should actually be handled first, so we could try `ordering = NULL`. However, we can also explicitly specify that rules with contextual information should be applied first by using `ordering = "context"`. That gives the right results for this toy example, as shown in Table 8.8.

```
# add a contextual grapheme, and then use the edited
# profile to tokenize
tokenize( example
        , profile = "~/Desktop/profile_skeleton.txt"
        , regex = TRUE
```

[26]The column names `Left`, `Right` and `Grapheme` are currently hard-coded, so these exact column names should be used for these effects to take place. The position of the columns in the profile is unimportant. So the column `Left` can occur anywhere.

```
    , ordering = "context"
  )$strings

##    originals      tokenized
## 1    shampoo    sh a m p oo
## 2     mishap    m i s h a p
## 3   mischief m i s ch ie f
## 4     scheme     s ch e m e
```

Table 8.8: Orthography profile with contextual specification for <s>

Left	Grapheme	Frequency	Codepoint	UnicodeName
mi	s			
	sh			
	ch			
	sch			
	ie			
	oo			
	a	2	U+0061	LATIN SMALL LETTER A
	c	2	U+0063	LATIN SMALL LETTER C
	e	3	U+0065	LATIN SMALL LETTER E
	f	1	U+0066	LATIN SMALL LETTER F
	h	4	U+0068	LATIN SMALL LETTER H
	i	3	U+0069	LATIN SMALL LETTER I
	m	4	U+006D	LATIN SMALL LETTER M
	o	2	U+006F	LATIN SMALL LETTER O
	p	2	U+0070	LATIN SMALL LETTER P
	s	4	U+0073	LATIN SMALL LETTER S

Note that with the option `regex = TRUE` all content in the profile is treated as regular expressions, so the characters with special meaning in regular expressions should be either omitted or escaped (by putting a < \ > REVERSE SOLIDUS at U+005C before the character). Specifically, this concerns the following characters:

<-> HYPHEN-MINUS at U+002D
<!> EXCLAMATION MARK at U+0021
<?> QUESTION MARK at U+003F
<.> FULL STOP at U+002E
<(> LEFT PARENTHESIS at U+0028
<)> RIGHT PARENTHESIS at U+0029
<[> LEFT SQUARE BRACKET at U+005B
<]> RIGHT SQUARE BRACKET at U+005D
<{> LEFT CURLY BRACKET at U+007B

<}> RIGHT CURLY BRACKET at U+007D
<|> VERTICAL LINE at U+007C
<*> ASTERISK at U+002A
<\> REVERSE SOLIDUS at U+005C
<^> CIRCUMFLEX ACCENT at U+005E
<+> PLUS SIGN at U+002B
<$> DOLLAR SIGN at U+0024

Profile skeleton with columns for editing

When it is expected that context might be important for a profile, then the profile skeleton can be created with columns prepared for the contextual specifications. This is done by using the option `editing = TRUE` (cf. Table 8.9 for a toy profile of some Italian words).

```
example <- c('cane', 'cena', 'cine')
write.profile(example
             , file = "~/Desktop/profile_skeleton.txt"
             , editing = TRUE
             , info = FALSE
             )
```

Table 8.9: Orthography profile with empty columns for editing contexts

Left	Grapheme	Right	Class	Replacement
	a			a
	c			c
	e			e
	i			i
	n			n

Besides the columns `Left`, `Grapheme`, and `Right` as discussed in the previous sections, there are also columns `Class` and `Replacement`. The column `Class` can be used to specify classes of graphemes that can then be used in the contextual specification. The column `Replacement` is just a copy of the column `Grapheme`, providing a skeleton to specify transliteration. The name of the column `Replacement` is not fixed – there can actually be multiple columns with different kinds of transliterations in a single profile.

To achieve contextually determined replacements it is possible to use a regular expression in the contextual column. For example, consider the edited toy

Table 8.10: Orthography profile with regex as context

Left	Grapheme	Right	Class	IPA
	c	[ie]		tʃ
	a			a
	n			n
	c			k
	e			e
	i			i

profile for Italian in Table 8.10 (where <c> becomes /k/ except before <i,e>, then it becomes /tʃ/).

To use this profile, you have to add the option `regex = TRUE`. Also note that we have changed the name of the transliteration column, so we have to tell the tokenization process to use this column to transliterate. This is done by adding the option `transliterate = "IPA"`.

```
# add a contextual grapheme, and then use the edited
# profile to tokenize
tokenize( example
        , profile = "~/Desktop/profile_skeleton.txt"
        , regex = TRUE
        , transliterate = "IPA"
        )$strings
```

```
##   originals tokenized transliterated
## 1      cane   c a n e          k a n e
## 2      cena   c e n a         tʃ e n a
## 3      cine   c i n e         tʃ i n e
```

Another equivalent possibility is to use a column `Class` to specify a class of graphemes, and then use this class in the specification of context. This is useful to keep track of recurrent classes in larger profiles. You are free to use any class-name you like, as long as it does not clash with the rest of the profile. The example shown in Table 8.11 should give the same result as obtained previously by using a regular expression.

```
# add a class, and then use the edited profile to tokenize
tokenize( example
        , profile = "~/Desktop/profile_skeleton.txt"
        , regex = TRUE
        , transliterate = "IPA"
        )$strings
```

Table 8.11: Orthography profile with Class as context

Left	Grapheme	Right	Class	IPA
	c	Vfront		tʃ
	a			a
	n			n
	c			k
	e		Vfront	e
	i		Vfront	i

```
##   originals tokenized transliterated
## 1      cane   c a n e        k a n e
## 2      cena   c e n a       tʃ e n a
## 3      cine   c i n e       tʃ i n e
```

Formatting grapheme separation

In all examples above we have used the default formatting for grapheme separation using space as a separator, which is obtained by the default setting `sep = " "`. It is possible to specify any other separator here, including the empty string, i.e. `sep = ""`. This will not show the graphemic tokenization anymore (although it has of course been used in the background).

```
# Use the empty string as separator
tokenize( example
        , profile = "~/Desktop/profile_skeleton.txt"
        , regex = TRUE
        , transliterate = "IPA"
        , sep = ""
        )$strings
```

```
##   originals tokenized transliterated
## 1      cane      cane           kane
## 2      cena      cena          tʃena
## 3      cine      cine          tʃine
```

Normally, the separator specified should not occur in the data. If it does, unexpected things might happen, so consider removing the chosen separator from your strings first. However, there is also an option `sep.replace` to replace the separator with something else. When `sep.replace` is specified, this mark is inserted in the string at those places where the separator occurs. Typical usage in linguistics would be `sep = " ", sep.replace = "#"` adding spaces between graphemes and replacing spaces in the input string by hashes in the output string.

```
# Replace separator in string to be tokenized
tokenize( "test test test"
        , sep = " "
        , sep.replace = "#"
        )$strings$tokenized

## [1] "t e s t # t e s t # t e s t"
```

Remaining issues

Given a set of graphemes, there are at least two different methods to tokenize strings. The first is called `method = "global"`. This approach takes the first grapheme in the profile, then matches this grapheme globally at all places in the string, and then turns to process the next string in the profile. The other approach is called `method = "linear"`. This approach walks through the string from left to right. At the first character it looks through all graphemes whether there is any match, and then walks further to the end of the match and starts again. This approach is more akin to finite-state rewrite rules (though note that it still works differently from such rewrite rules, as previously stated). The global method is used by default in the R implementation.

In some special cases these two tokenization methods can lead to different results, but these special situations are very unlikely to happen in natural language. The example below shows that a string `'abc'` can be parsed differently in case of a very special profile with a very special ordering of the graphemes.

```
# different parsing methods can lead to different results
# the global method first catches 'bc'
tokenize( "abc"
        , profile = c("bc","ab","a","c")
        , order = NULL
        , method = "global"
        )$strings

##   originals tokenized
## 1       abc      a bc


# the linear method catches the first grapheme, which is 'ab'
tokenize( "abc"
        , profile = c("bc","ab","a","c")
        , order = NULL
        , method = "linear"
        )$strings
```

```
##   originals tokenized
## 1       abc      ab c
```

Further, the current R implementation has a limitation when regular expressions are used. The problem is that overlapping matches are not captured when using regular expressions.[27] Everything works as expected without regular expressions, but there might be warnings/errors in case of `regex = TRUE`. However, just as in the previous issue, this problem should only very rarely (when at all) happen in natural language data.

The problem can be exemplified by a sequence <bbbb> in which a grapheme <bb> should be matched. With the default `regex = FALSE` there are three possible matches, but with `regex = TRUE` only the first two <b>'s or the last two <b>'s are matched. The middle two <b>'s are not matched because they overlap with the other matches. In the example below this leads to an error, because the second <bb> is not matched. However, we have not been able to produce a real example in any natural language in which this limitation might lead to an error.

```
# Everything perfect without regular expressions
tokenize( "abbb"
        , profile = c("ab","bb")
        , order = NULL
        , regex = FALSE
        )$strings

##   originals tokenized
## 1      abbb     ab bb


# Matching with regular expressions does not catch overlap
tokenize( "abbb"
        , profile = c("ab","bb")
        , order = NULL
        , regex = TRUE
        )$strings

## Warning in tokenize("abbb", profile = c("ab", "bb"), order = NULL, regex = TRUE):
  ## There were unknown characters found in the input data.
  ## Check output$errors for a table with all problematic strings.

##   originals tokenized
## 1      abbb    ab ⁇ ⁇
```

[27]This restriction is an effect of the underlyingly used ICU implementation of the Unicode Standard as implemented in R through the package `stringi`.

8.5 Recipes online

We provide several use cases online – what we refer to as *recipes* – that illustrate the applications of orthography profiles using our implementations in Python and R.[28] Here we briefly describe these use cases and we encourage users to try them out using Git and Jupyter Notebooks.

First, as we discussed above, we provide a basic tutorial on how to use the Python `segments`[29] and R `qlcData`[30] libraries. This recipe simply shows the basic functions of each library to get you started.[31]

The two recipes using the Python `segments` package include a tutorial on how to segment graphemes in IPA text:

- https://github.com/unicode-cookbook/recipes/tree/master/JIPA

and an example of how to create an orthography profile to tokenize fieldwork data from a large comparative wordlist.

- https://github.com/unicode-cookbook/recipes/tree/master/Dogon

The JIPA recipes uses excerpts from *The North Wind and the Sun* passages from the Illustrations of the IPA published in the Journal of the International Phonetic Alphabet. Thus the recipe shows how a user might tokenize IPA proper. The Dogon recipe uses fieldwork data from the Dogon languages of Mali language documentation project.[32] This recipe illustrates how a user might tokenize fieldwork data from numerous linguists using different transcription practices by defining these practices with an orthography profile to make the output unified and comparable.

The two recipes using the R `qlcData` library include a use case for tokenizing wordlist data from the Automated Similarity Judgment Program (ASJP):[33]

- https://github.com/unicode-cookbook/recipes/tree/master/ASJP

and for tokenizing a corpus of text in Dutch orthography:

- https://github.com/unicode-cookbook/recipes/tree/master/Dutch

[28] https://github.com/unicode-cookbook/recipes
[29] https://pypi.python.org/pypi/segments
[30] https://github.com/cysouw/qlcData
[31] https://github.com/unicode-cookbook/recipes/tree/master/Basics
[32] http://dogonlanguages.org/
[33] http://asjp.clld.org/

The ASJP use case shows how to download the full set of ASJP wordlists, to combine them into a single large CSV file, and to tokenize the ASJP orthography. The Dutch use case takes as input the 10K corpus for Dutch ("nld") from the Leipzig Corpora Collection,[34] which is then cleaned and tokenized with an orthography profile that captures the intricacies of Dutch orthography.

[34] http://wortschatz.uni-leipzig.de/en/download/

References

Abercrombie, David. 1964. *English phonetic texts*. London: Faber & Faber LTD.

Anderson, Lloyd B. 1984. Multilingual text processing in a two-byte code. In *Proceedings of the 10th International Conference on Computational Linguistics*, 1–4. Stanford, CA: Association for Computational Linguistics. http://dx.doi.org/10.3115/980431.980492. DOI:10.3115/980431.980492

Apple Computer. 1985. The font manager. *Inside Machintosh* 1. 215–240.

Apple Computer. 1986. The font manager. *Inside Machintosh* 4. 27–46.

Apple Computer. 1988. The script manager. *Inside Machintosh* 5. 293–322.

Becker, Joseph D. 1984. Multilingual word processing. *Scientific American* 251(1). 96–107. http://www.jstor.org/stable/24969416.

Beider, Alexander & Stephen P. Morse. 2008. Beider-Morse phonetic matching: An alternative to Soundex with fewer false hits. *Avotaynu: the International Review of Jewish Genealogy* 24(2). 12.

Belongie, Serge, Jitendra Malik & Jan Puzicha. 2002. Shape matching and object recognition using shape contexts. *IEEE Transactions on Pattern Analysis and Machine Intelligence* 24(4). 509–522. http://www.dtic.mil/get-tr-doc/pdf?AD=ADA640016. DOI:10.1109/34.993558

Bird, Steven & Gary F. Simons. 2003. Seven dimensions of portability for language documentation and description. *Language* 79(3). 557–582. DOI:https://doi.org/10.1353/lan.2003.0149

Brindle, Jonathan. 2017. *A dictionary and grammatical outline of Chakali*. Vol. 2 (African Language Grammars and Dictionaries). Berlin: Language Science Press. DOI:https://doi.org/10.5281/zenodo.344813

Brown, Cecil H., Eric W. Holman & Søren Wichmann. 2013. Sound correspondences in the world's languages. *Language* 89(1). 4–29. DOI:10.1353/lan.2013.0009

Chao, Yuen Ren. 1930. A system of tone letters. *Le Maître Phonétique* 30. 24–27.

Cysouw, Michael. 2018. *cysouw/qlcData: Zenodo release (Version v0.2.1.0)*. Zenodo. https://github.com/cysouw/qlcData/tree/v0.2.1.0. DOI:http://doi.org/10.5281/zenodo.1137278

Daniels, Peter T. 1990. Fundamentals of grammatology. *Journal of the American Oriental Society* 110(4). 727–731. http://www.jstor.org/stable/602899. DOI:10.2307/602899

Daniels, Peter T. 1996. The study of writing systems. In P. T. Daniels & W. Bright (eds.), *The world's writing systems*. New York, NY: Oxford University Press.

Daniels, Peter T. & William Bright. 1996. *The world's writing systems*. New York, NY: Oxford University Press.

Dolgopolsky, Aharon B. 1986. A probabilistic hypothesis concerning the oldest relationships among the language families of Northern Eurasia. In Vitalij V. Shevoroshkin & Thomas L. Markey (eds.), *Typology, relationship and time: a collection of papers on language change and relationship by soviet linguists*, 27–50. Ann Arbor, MI: Karoma.

Duckworth, Martin, George Allen, William Hardcastle & Martin Ball. 1990. Extensions to the International Phonetic Alphabet for the transcription of atypical speech. *Clinical Linguistics & Phonetics* 4(4). 273–280. DOI:https://doi.org/10.3109/02699209008985489

Esling, John H. 1990. Computer coding of the IPA: supplementary report. *Journal of the International Phonetic Association* 20(1). 22–26.

Esling, John H. & Harry Gaylord. 1993. Computer codes for phonetic symbols. *Journal of the International Phonetic Association* 23(2). 83–97.

Evans, Nicholas & Stephen C. Levinson. 2009. The myth of language universals: language diversity and its importance for cognitive science. *Behavioral and Brain Sciences* 32(5). 429–448.

Forkel, Robert & Steven Moran. 2018. *cldf/segments: Unicode Standard tokenization (Version v1.2.2)*. Zenodo. https://github.com/cldf/segments/tree/v1.2.2. DOI:http://doi.org/10.5281/zenodo.1296127

Gaultney, J. Victor. 2002. *Problems of diacritic design for Latin script text faces*. Reading, UK MA thesis. https://www.sil.org/resources/archives/9816.

Hieronymus, James L. 1993. ASCII phonetic symbols for the world's languages: Worldbet. *Journal of the International Phonetic Association* 23.

Huurdeman, Anton A. 2003. *The worldwide history of telecommunications*. New York, NY: John Wiley & Sons.

Kemp, Alan. 2006. Phonetic transcription: history. *The Encyclopedia of Language and Linguistics* 6. 396–410.

Knuth, Donald E. 1973. *The art of programming: sorting and searching*. Vol. 3. Reading, MA: Addison-Wesley.

Kohrt, Manfred. 1986. The term 'grapheme' in the history and theory of linguistics. In Gerhard Augst (ed.), *New trends in graphemics and orthography*, 80–96. Berlin: de Gruyter.

Ladefoged, Peter. 1990. Some reflections on the IPA. *Journal of Phonetics* 18(3). 335–346.

List, Johann-Mattis. 2012. SCA: phonetic alignment based on sound classes. In Daniel Lassiter & Marija Slavkovik (eds.), *New directions in logic, language, and computation*, 32–51. Berlin & Heidelberg: Springer.

Maddieson, Ian. 1984. *Patterns of sounds*. Cambridge, UK: Cambridge University Press.

Maddieson, Ian. 1990. The transcription of tone in the IPA. *Journal of the International Phonetic Association* 20(2). 28–32.

Maddieson, Ian & Kristin Precoda. 1990. Updating UPSID. In *UCLA working papers in phonetics*, vol. 74, 104–111. Department of Linguistics, UCLA.

Maddieson, Ian & Kristin Precoda. 1992. *UPSID and PHONEME*. User manual. http://phonetics.linguistics.ucla.edu/sales/UPSID-guide.pdf.

Mania, Hubert. 2008. *Gauss: eine Biographie*. Reinbek bei Hamburg: Rowohlt.

McLaughlin, Fiona. 2005. Voiceless implosives in Seereer-Siin. *Journal of the International Phonetic Association* 35(2). 201–214.

Meinhof, Carl & Daniel Jones. 1928. Principles of practical orthography for African languages. *Africa: Journal of the International African Institute* 1(2). 228–239.

Meyer, Julien. 2015. *Whistled languages: a worldwide inquiry on human whistled speech*. Berlin: Springer.

Meyer, Julien, Laure Dentel & Frank Seifart. 2012. A methodology for the study of rhythm in drummed forms of languages: application to Bora Manguaré of Amazon. In *Proceedings of Interspeech*, 687–690.

Mielke, Jeff. 2009. Segment inventories. *Language and Linguistics Compass* 3(2). 700–718. DOI:https://doi.org/10.1111/j.1749-818X.2008.00117.x

Moran, Steven. 2006. *A grammatical sketch of Western Sisaala*. Ypsilanti, MI: Eastern Michigan University MA thesis. http://commons.emich.edu/theses/73/.

Moran, Steven. 2012. *Phonetics information base and lexicon*. University of Washington dissertation. https://digital.lib.washington.edu/researchworks/handle/1773/22452.

Moran, Steven & Daniel McCloy. 2014. *PHOIBLE notational conventions*. http://phoible.github.io/conventions/.

Moran, Steven, Daniel McCloy & Richard Wright (eds.). 2014. *PHOIBLE online*. Leipzig: Max Planck Institute for Evolutionary Anthropology. http://phoible.org/.

Olúmúyìw, Tèmítọ́pẹ́. 2013. Yoruba writing: standards and trends. *Journal of Arts and Humanities* 2(1). 40–51. http://www.theartsjournal.org/index.php/site/article/view/50.

Postel, Hans J. 1969. Die Kölner Phonetik: ein Verfahren zur Identifizierung von Personennamen auf der Grundlage der Gestaltanalyse. *IBM-Nachrichten* 19. 925–931.

Powell, Barry B. 2012. *Writing theory and history of the technology of civilization*. New York, NY: John Wiley & Sons.

Pullum, Geoffrey K. & William A. Ladusaw. 1986. *Phonetic symbol guide*. Chicago, IL: University of Chicago Press.

Roach, P. J. 1989. Report on the 1989 Kiel convention. *Journal of the International Phonetic Association* 19(2). 67–80.

Robinson, Andrew. 1995. *The story of writing*. London: Thames & Hudson.

Sampson, Geoffrey. 1985. *Writing systems*. Stanford, CA: Stanford University Press.

Simons, Gary F. 1989. Working with special characters. In Priscilla M. Kew & Gary F. Simons (eds.), *Laptop publishing for the field linguist: an approach based on Microsoft Word* (Occasional Publications in Academic Computing), 103–118. Dallas, TX: Summer Institute of Linguistics. https://www.sil.org/resources/archives/1483.

Simons, Gary F. 1996. The nature of linguistic data and the requirements of a computing environment for linguistic research. *Dutch Studies on Near Eastern Languages and Literature* 2(1). 111–128.

Singh, Simon. 1999. *The code book*. New York, NY: Doubleday.

Sproat, Richard. 2000. *A computational theory of writing systems*. Cambridge, UK: Cambridge University Press.

The International Phonetic Association. 1949. *The principles of the IPA*. London: International Phonetic Association.

The International Phonetic Association. 1999. *Handbook of the International Phonetic Association: a guide to the use of the International Phonetic Alphabet*. Cambridge, UK: Cambridge University Press.

The International Phonetic Association. 2015. *The International Phonetic Association*. https://www.internationalphoneticassociation.org.

The Unicode Consortium. 2018. *The Unicode Standard, version 11.0.0*. Tech. rep. Mountain View, CA: The Unicode Consortium. http://www.unicode.org/versions/Unicode11.0.0/.

Vidal, Alejandra. 2001. *Pilagá grammar (Guaykuruan family, Argentina)*. University of Oregon dissertation.

Wells, John C. 1987. Computer-coded phonetic transcription. *Journal of the International Phonetic Association* 17(2). 94–114.

Wells, John C. 1995. Computer-coding the IPA: a proposed extension of SAMPA. http://www.phon.ucl.ac.uk/home/sampa/ipasam-x.pdf.

Wells, John C., William Barry, Martine Grice, Adrian Fourcin & Dafydd Gibbon. 1992. Standard computer-compatible transcription. *Esprit project 2589 (SAM), Doc. no. SAM-UCL 37*.

Name index